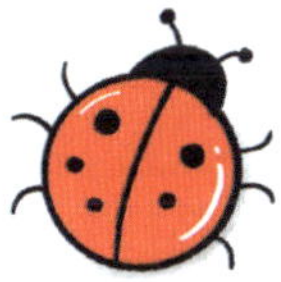

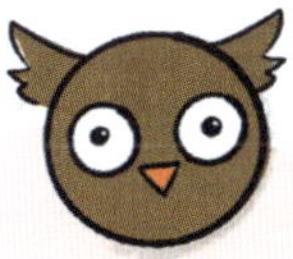

Drawing Simple Things from CIRCLES

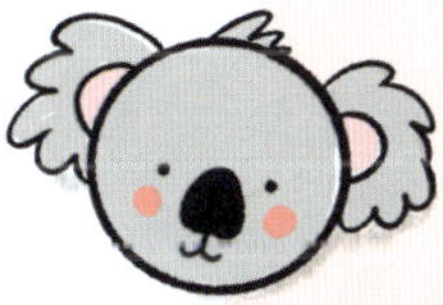

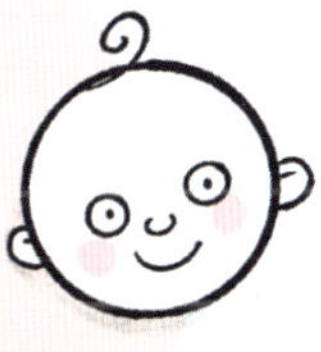

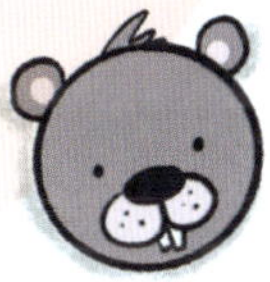

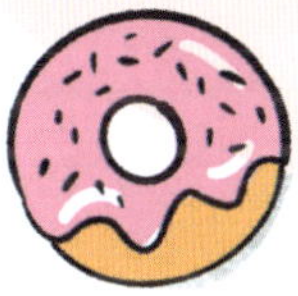

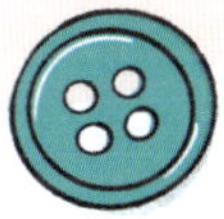

AF794677

Smith Street Books

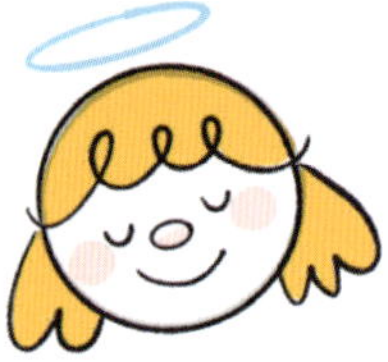
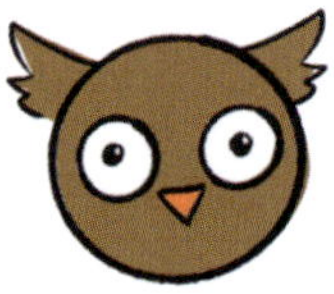
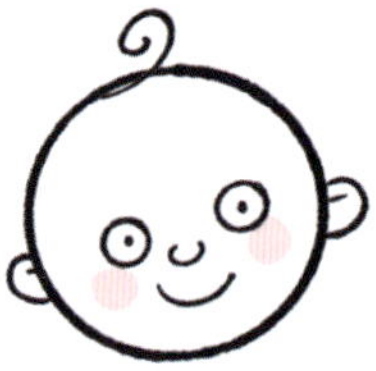
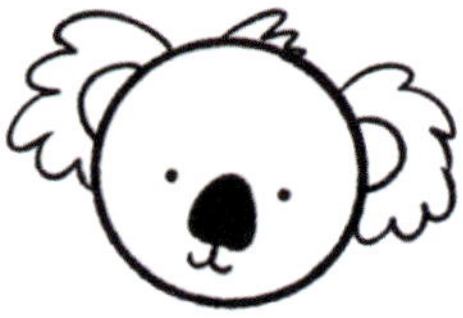
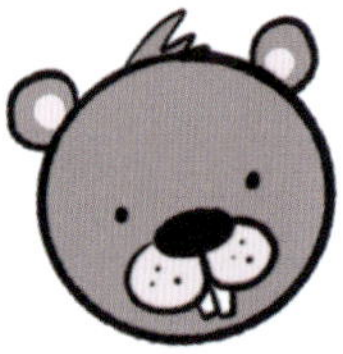
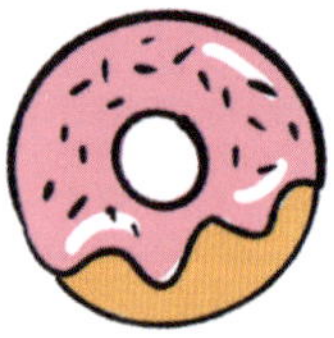
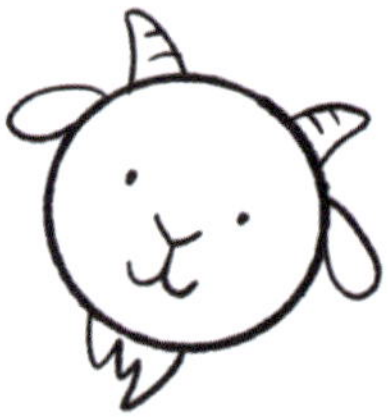
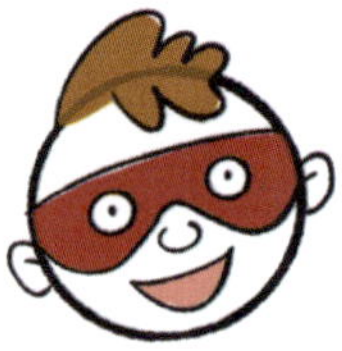

CONTENTS

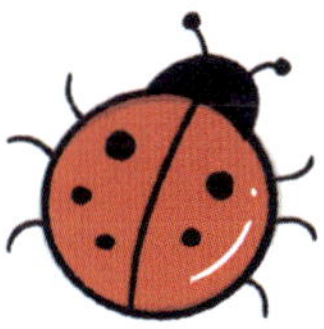

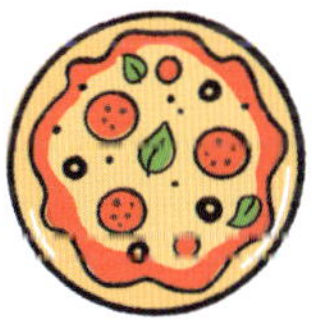

A round HELLO!

In my many years of drawing and teaching, I've noticed that for simple (and therefore quick) sketching, it really helps to reduce things to simple shapes. This is especially useful for quick visualisation – if you're drawing something on a flip chart, for example. The simpler the picture is, the faster it can be drawn. This principle is called the Visual Alphabet. It breaks down objects to basic shapes – circles, lines, triangles and squares – so you can draw them quickly.

A fun creative exercise often used in drawing workshops is to give participants a sheet of empty circles, and then ask them to turn them into something. But I've found that for many people, this isn't easy, as not everyone sees things in simple shapes. And that's how the idea for this book came about.

As you'll learn in this book, you can draw lots of things using simple circles. While it can be tricky to draw good circles freehand (unless you have a compass handy), you don't need to worry – they'll never be perfectly round – and they don't have to be.

Have fun drawing!

Nadine

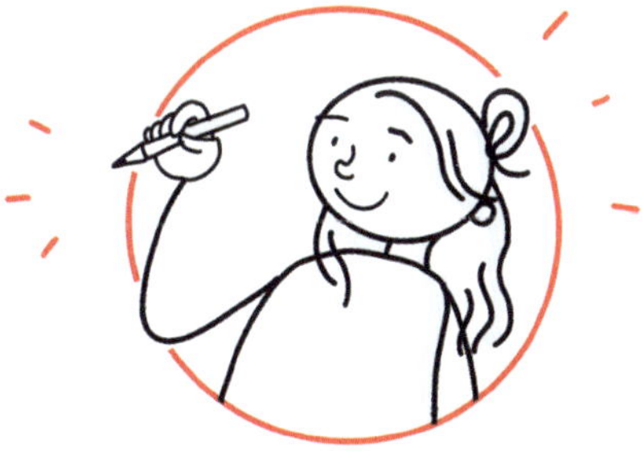

Nadine Rossa lives and works as an illustrator in Berlin. After working as a screen designer in Cologne, she studied communication design in Berlin and Helsinki. Since then, she has worked as a visualisation expert, helping anyone who wants to achieve quick results with visualisation and doodles, both professionally and privately, and who wants to present their ideas visually. After having her books published in her native German, she's delighted to bring them to an English-speaking audience.

You can find Nadine Rossa at:
www.sketchnote-love.com

CHAPTER 1

Animals

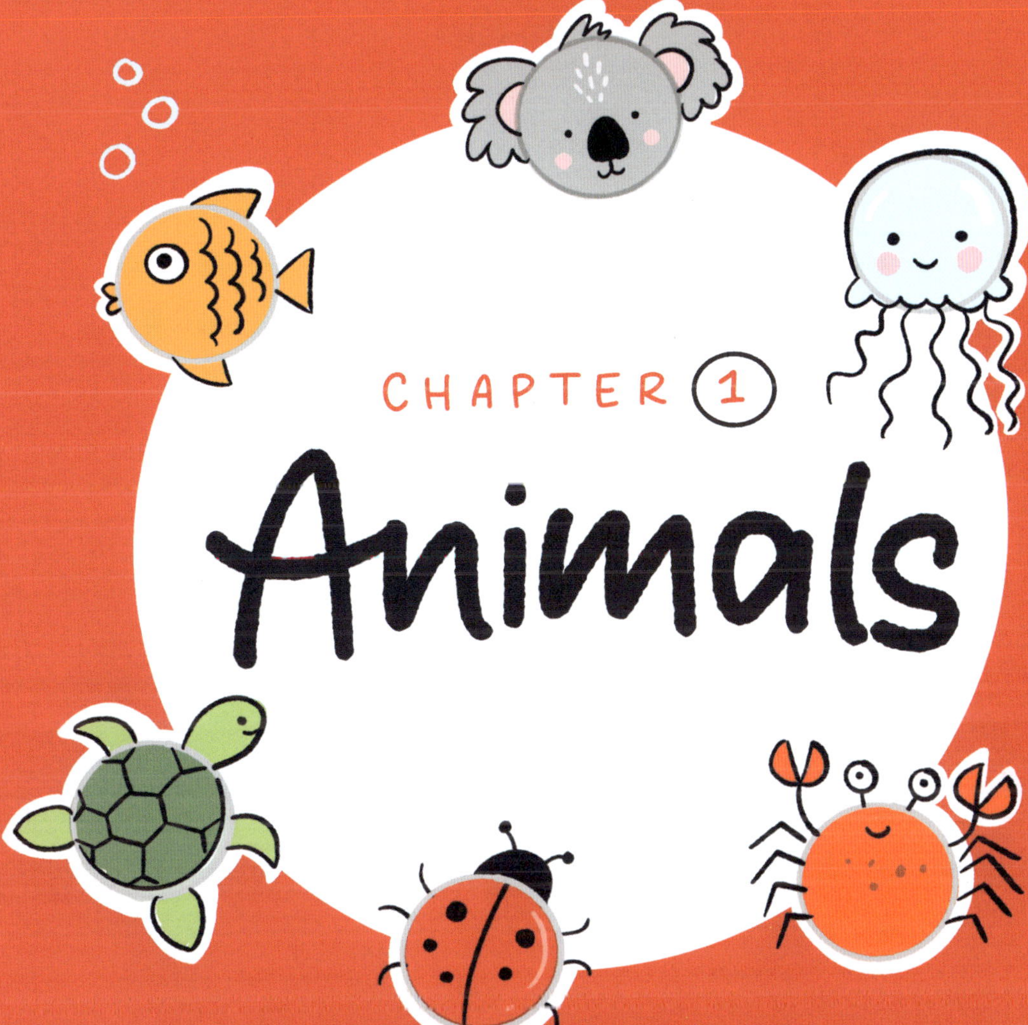

Fish

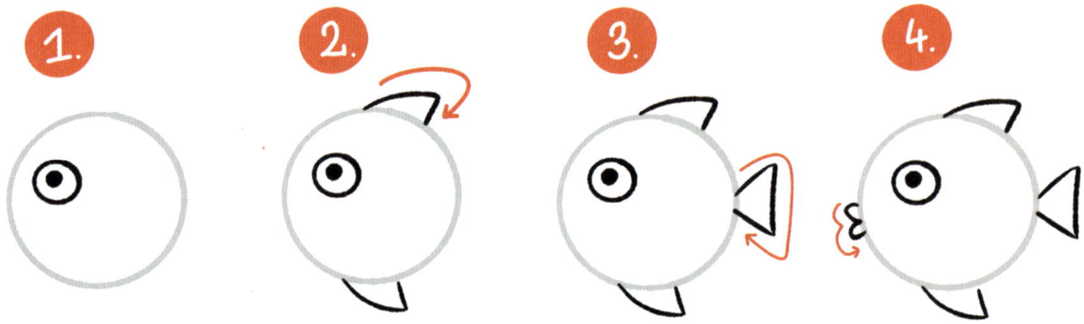
1.
2.
3.
4.

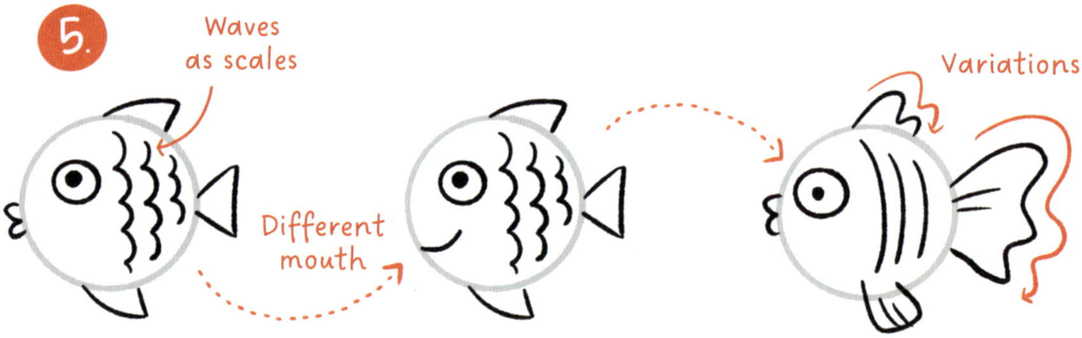
5.
Waves as scales
Different mouth
Variations

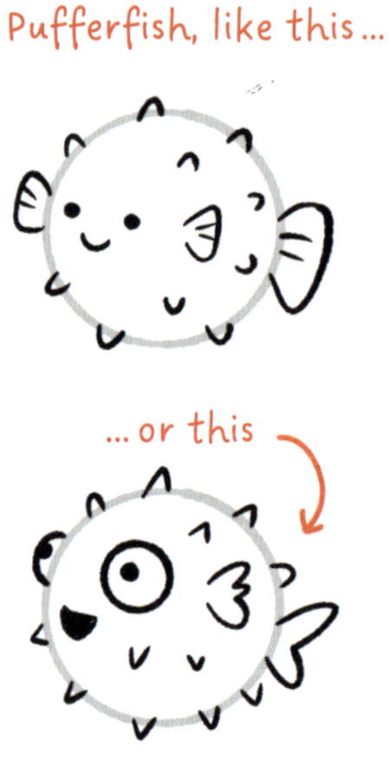
Pufferfish, like this...
...or this

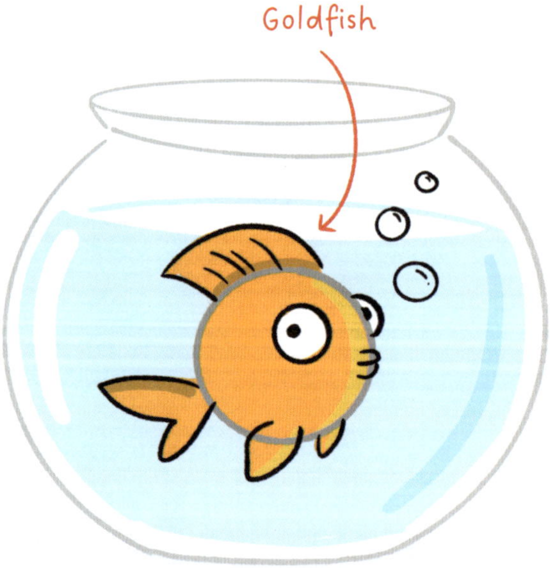
Goldfish

Turtle

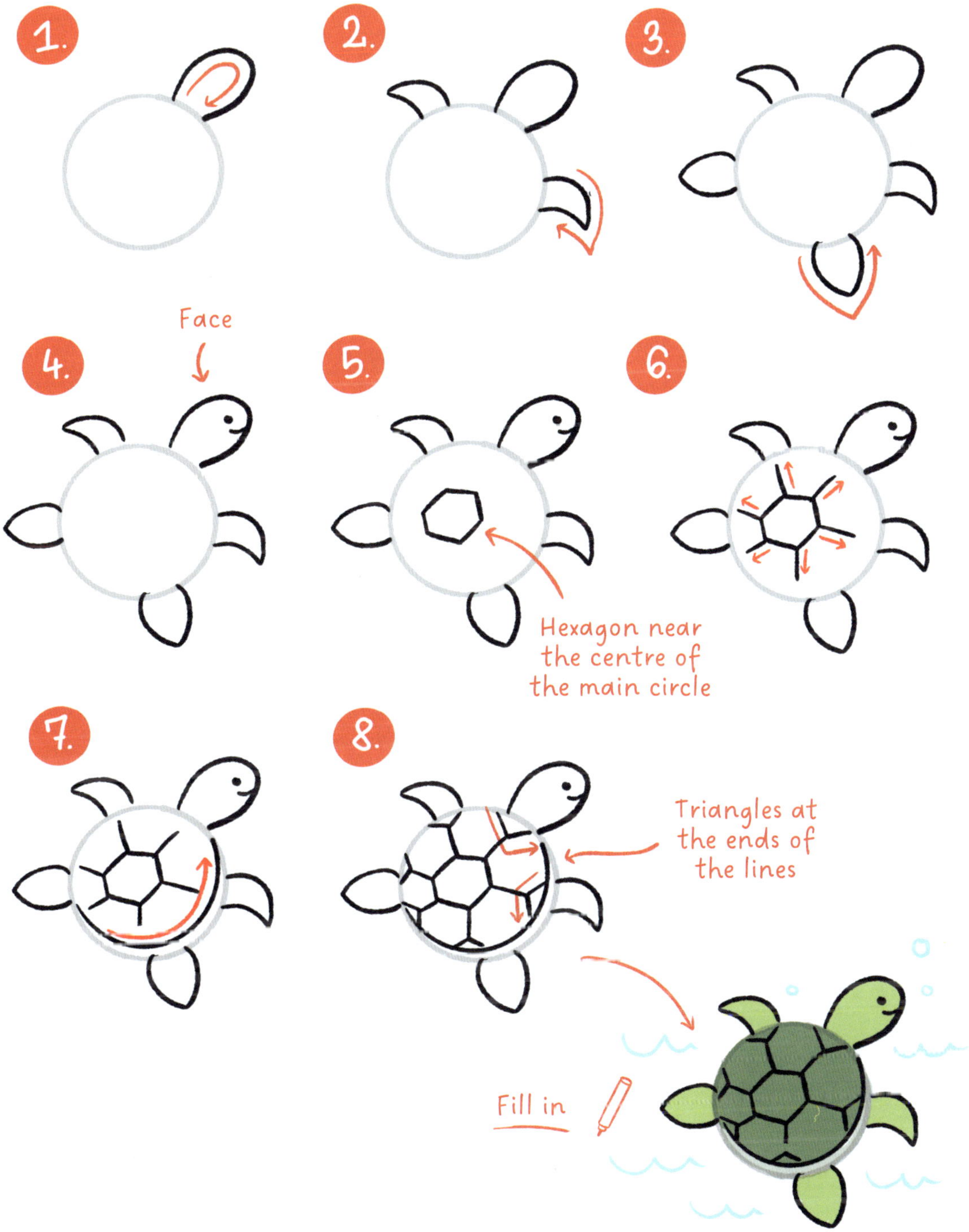
1.
2.
3.
Face
4.
5.
6.
Hexagon near the centre of the main circle
7.
8.
Triangles at the ends of the lines
Fill in

Octopus

1.

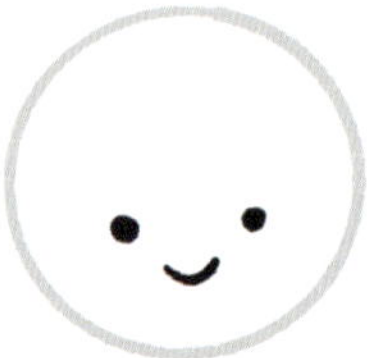

2.

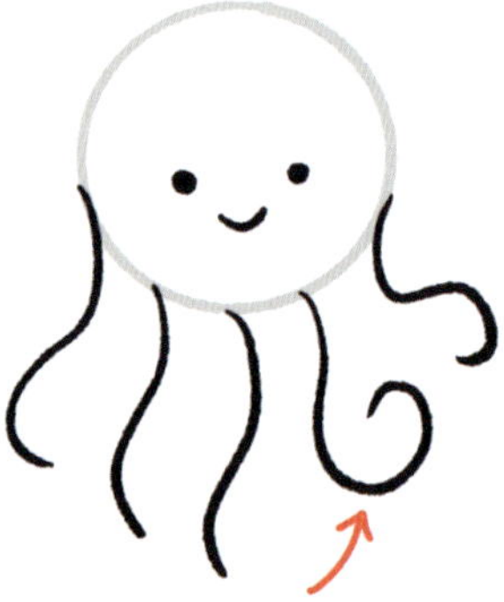

Draw tentacles

3.

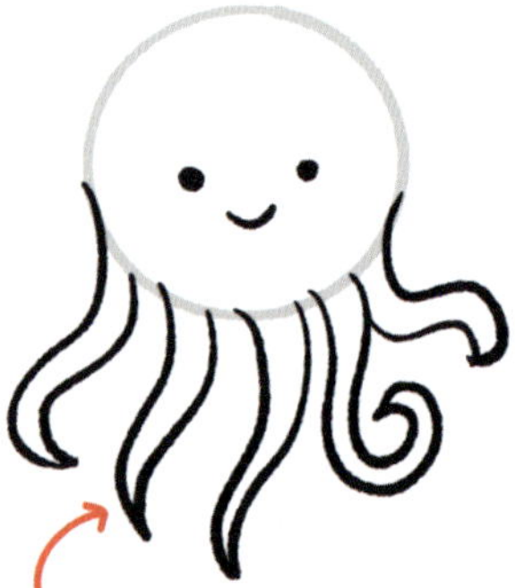

Pair each tentacle with a second line, joining at the end

4.

Fast version

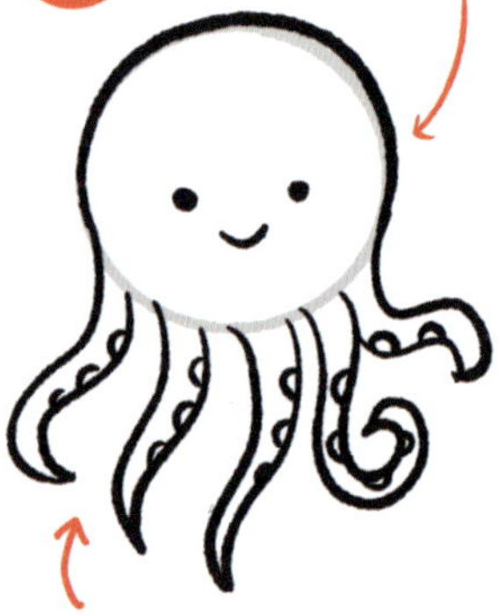

Complete the tentacles by adding suckers

More correct version

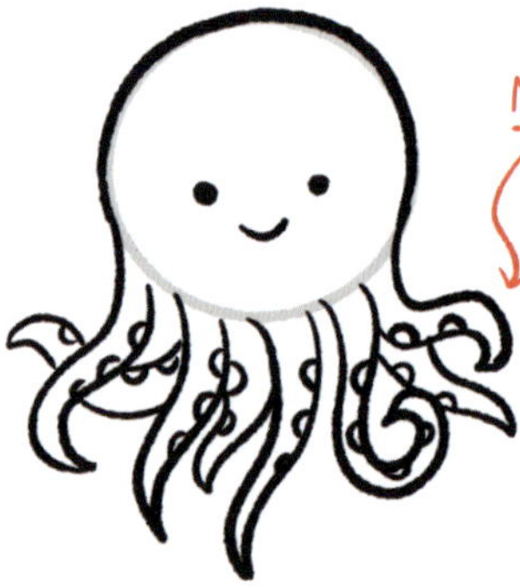

Draw eight tentacles, but then it gets quite crowded and hectic

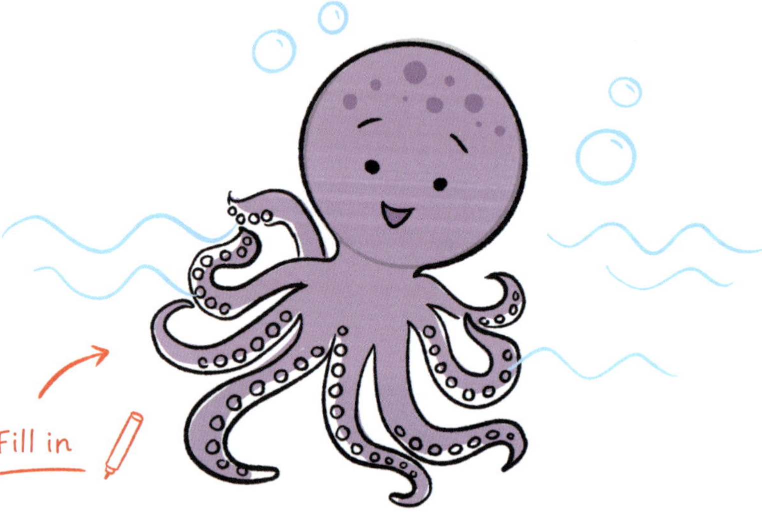

Fill in

Crab

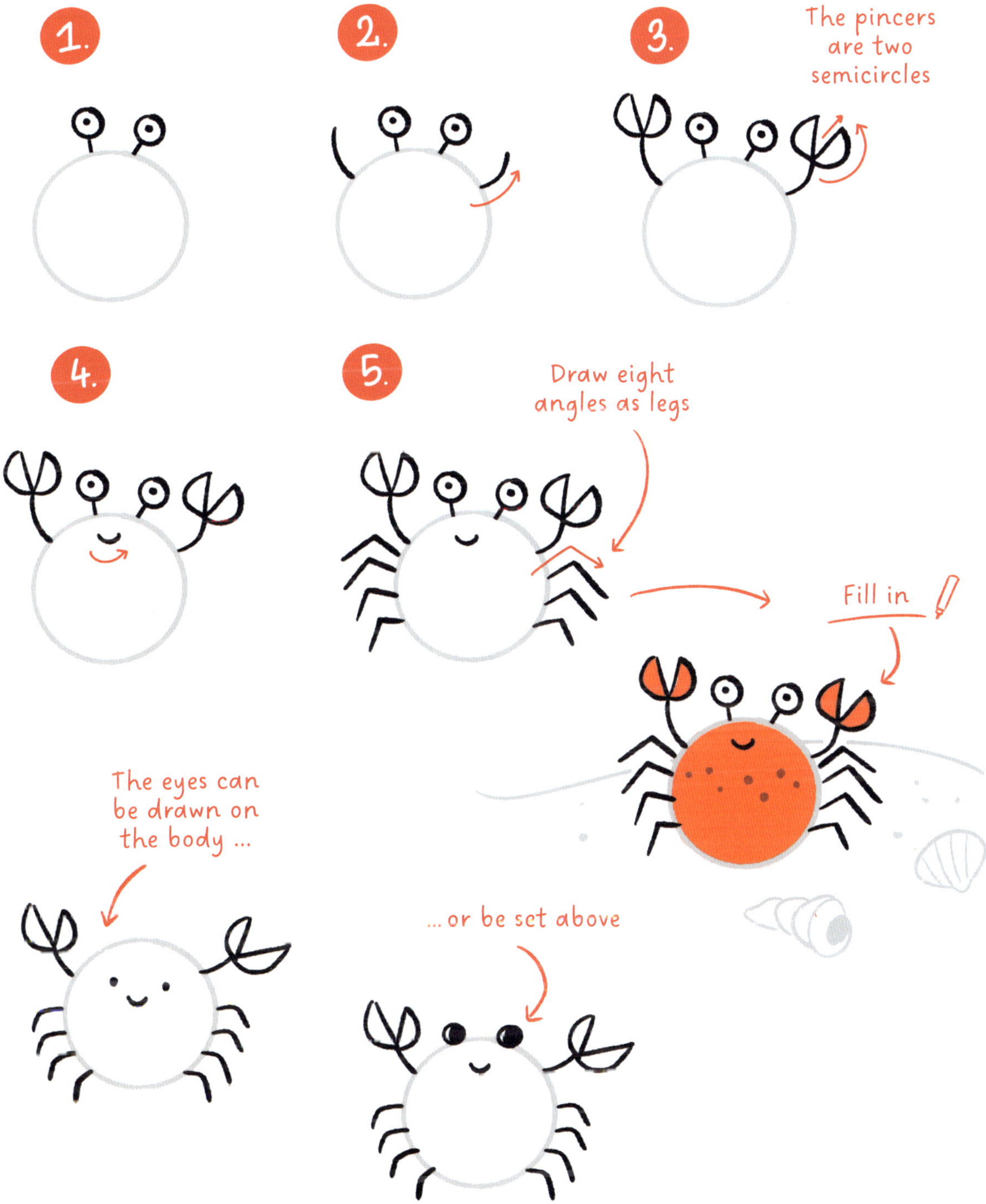
1.
2.
3.
The pincers are two semicircles
4.
5.
Draw eight angles as legs
Fill in
The eyes can be drawn on the body ...
... or be set above

Jellyfish

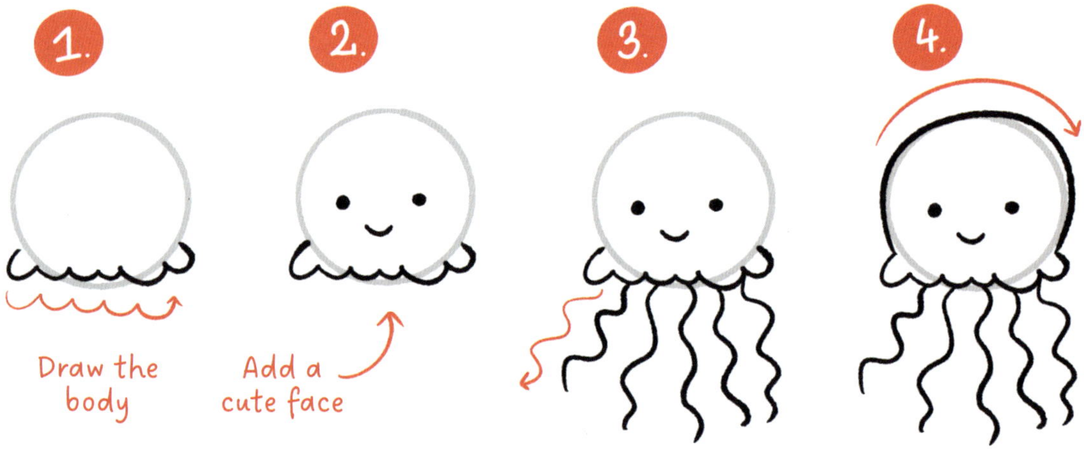

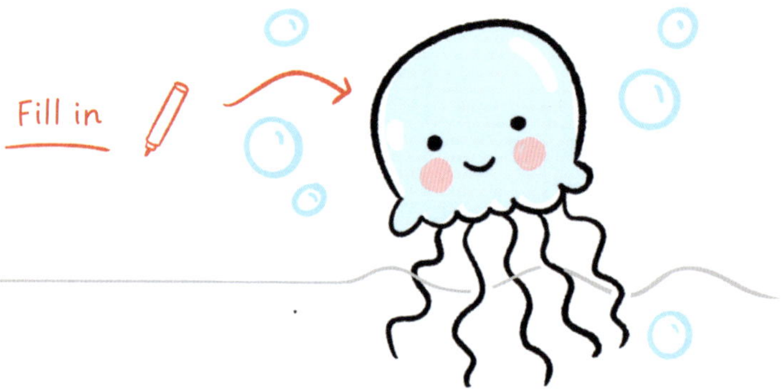

Duck

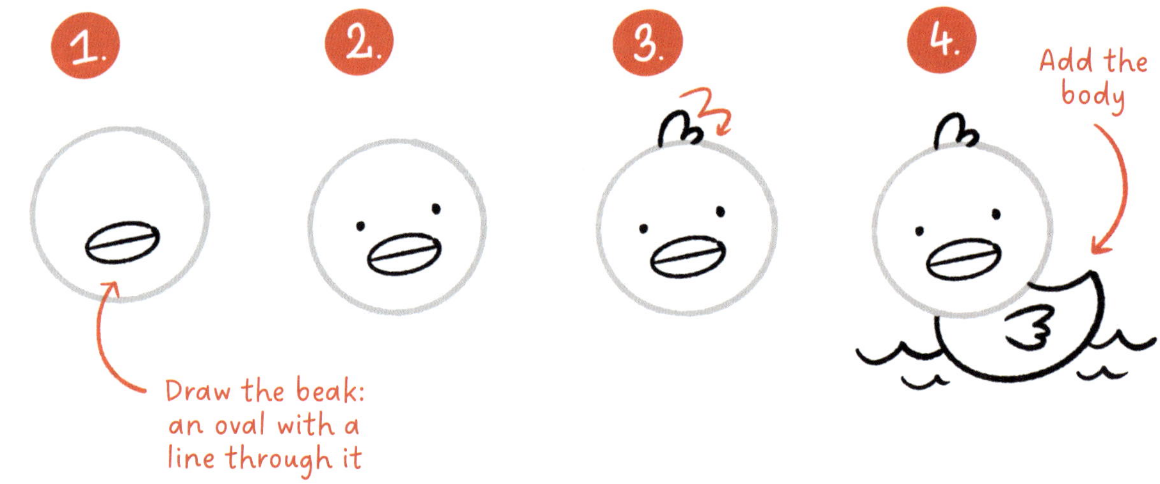

Frog

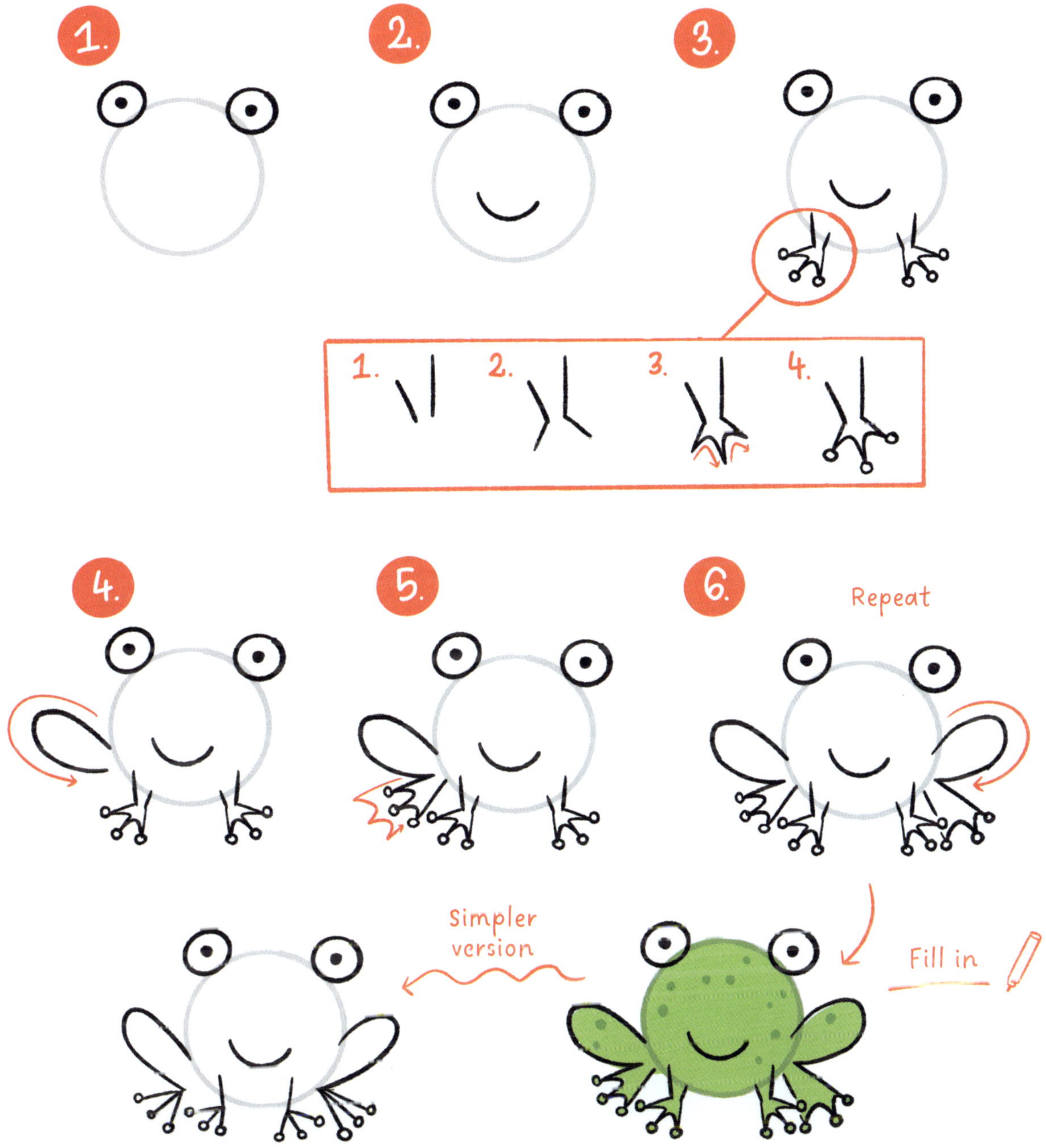

Axolotl

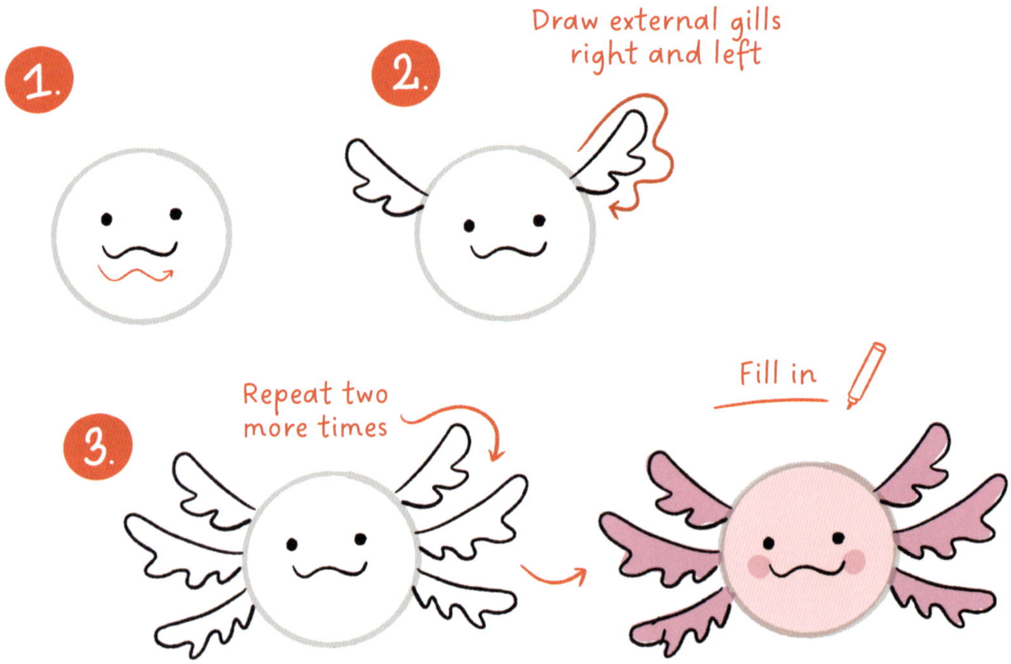
1.
2.
Draw external gills right and left
3.
Repeat two more times
Fill in

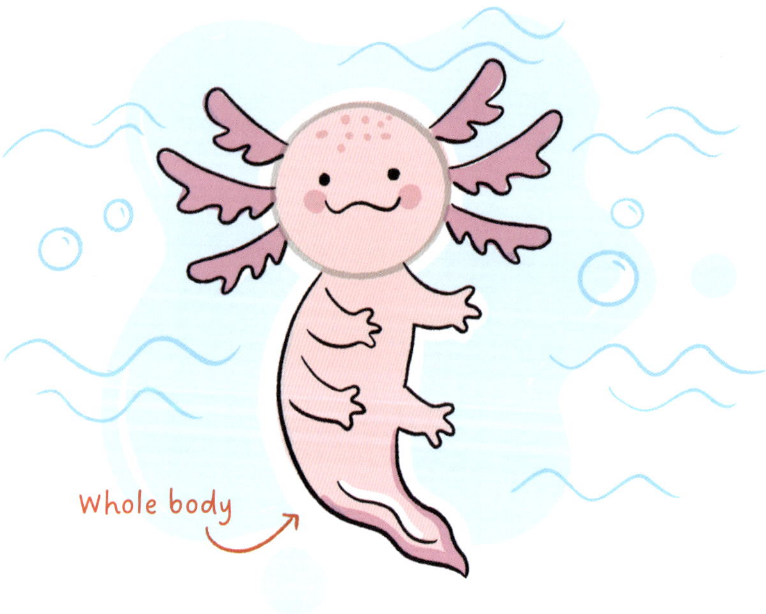
Whole body

Bat

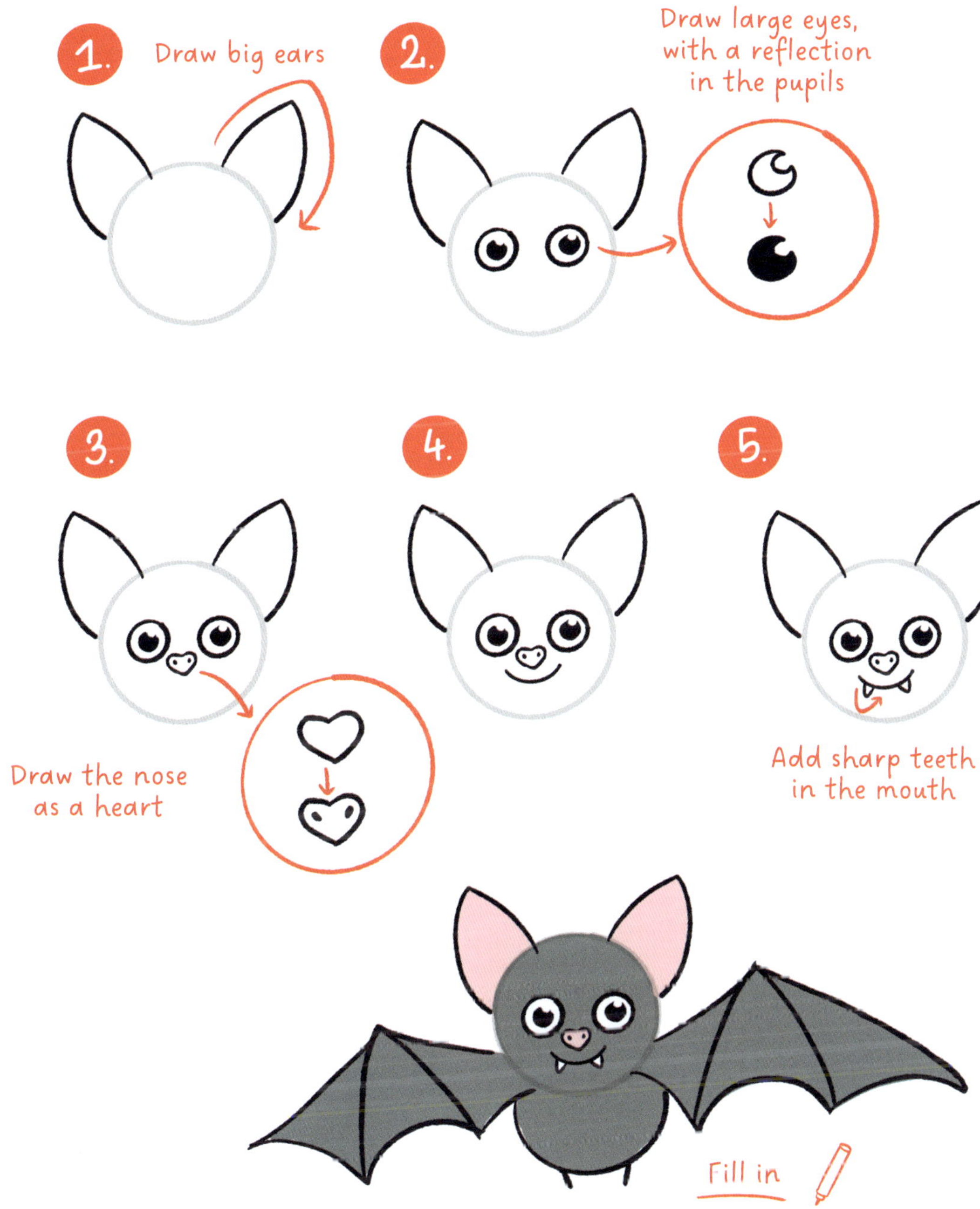
1.
Draw big ears
2.
Draw large eyes, with a reflection in the pupils
3.
Draw the nose as a heart
4.
5.
Add sharp teeth in the mouth
Fill in

Dog

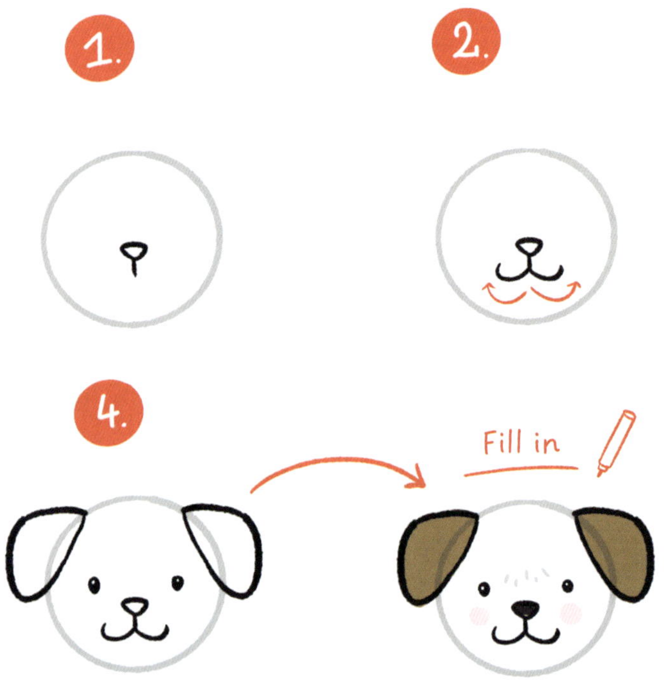

A few variations

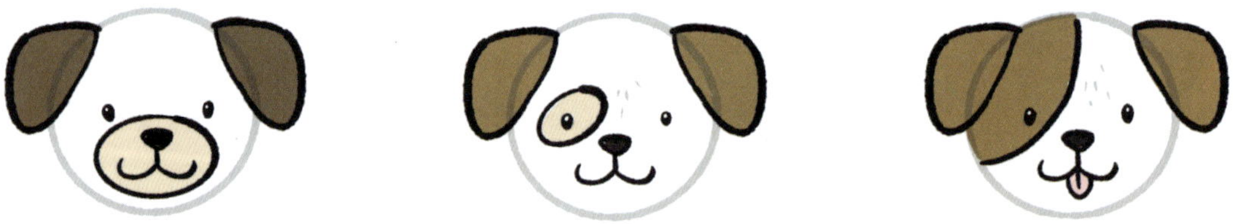

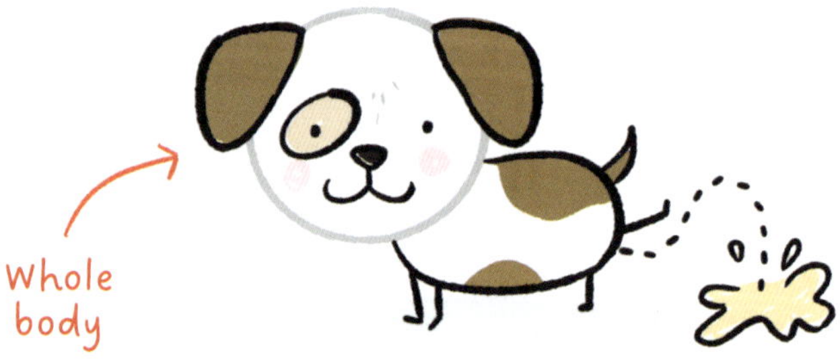

Other dog breeds

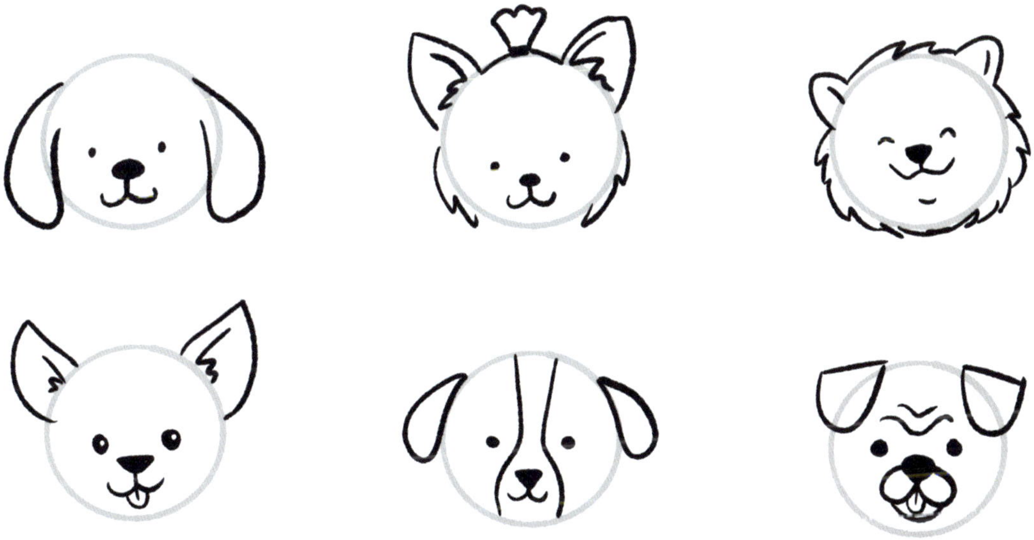

Cat

1.

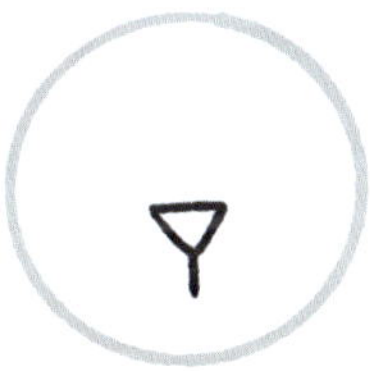

2.

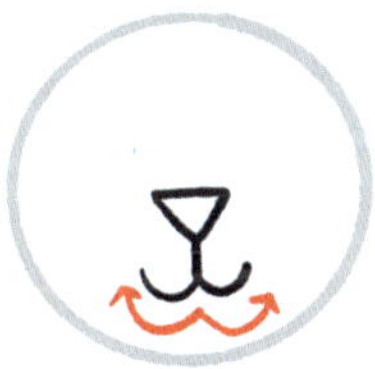

3.

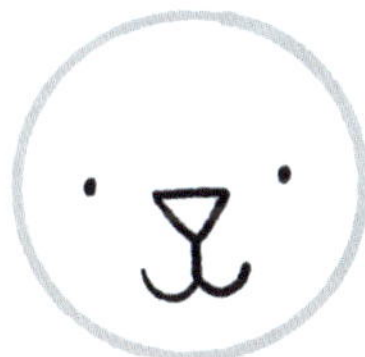

4.

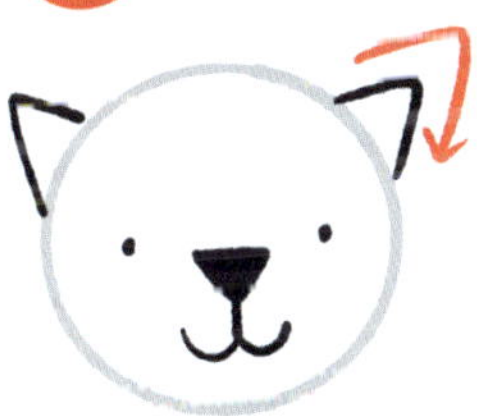

5.

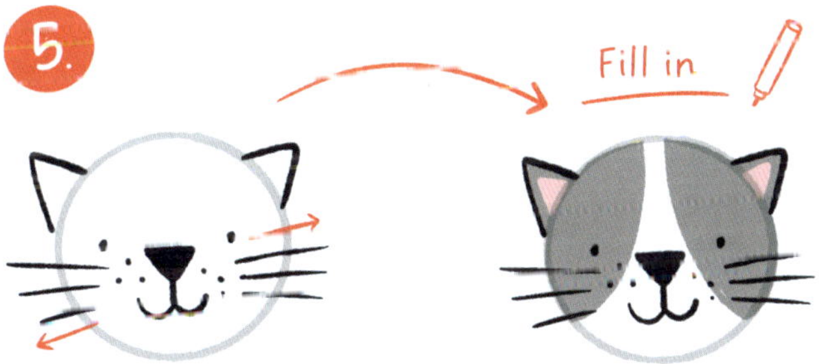

Bird

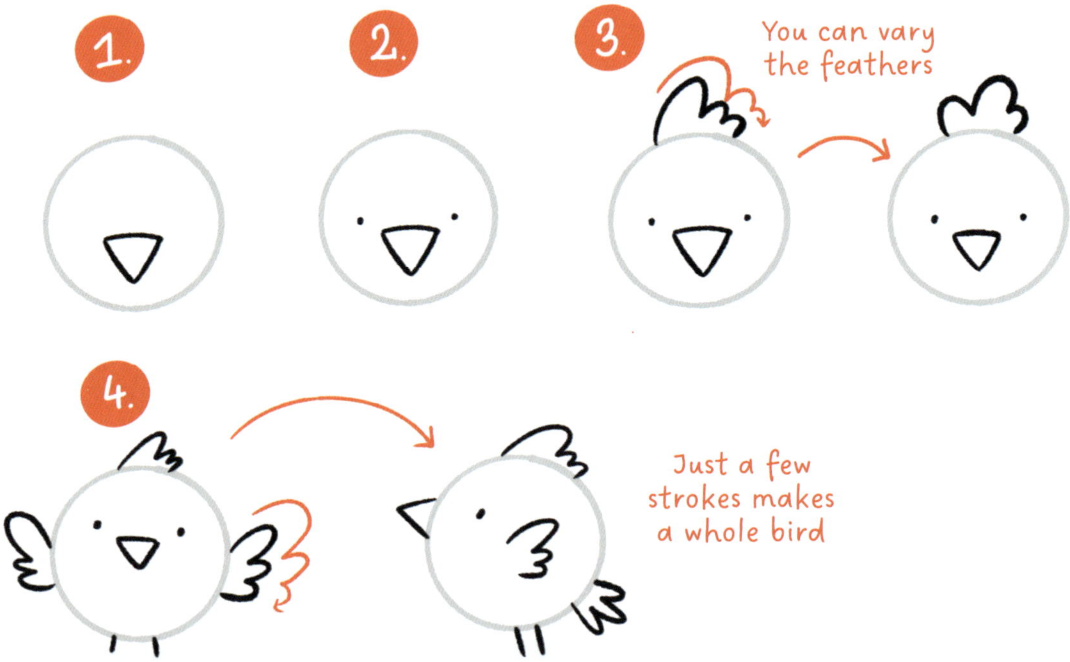
1.
2.
3.
You can vary the feathers
4.
Just a few strokes makes a whole bird

Owl

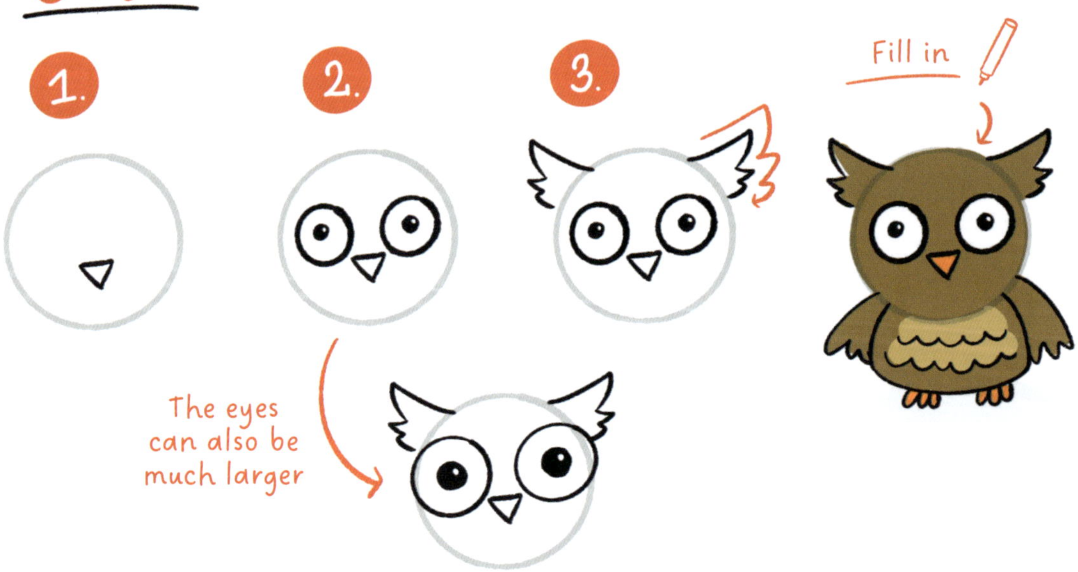
1.
2.
3.
Fill in
The eyes can also be much larger

Penguin

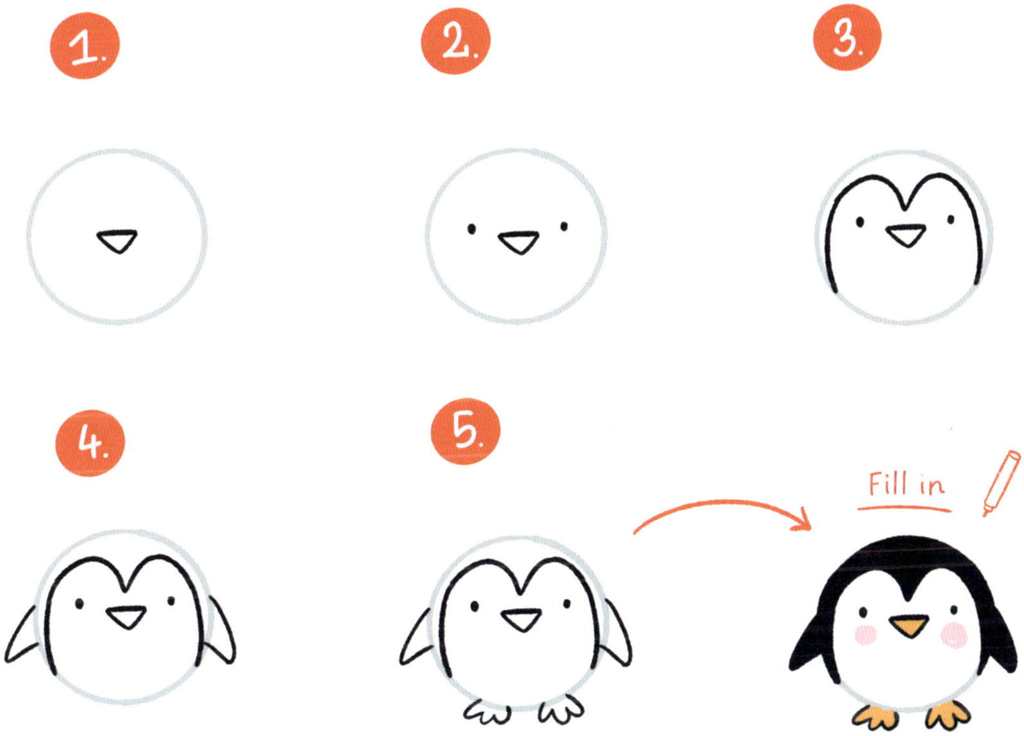

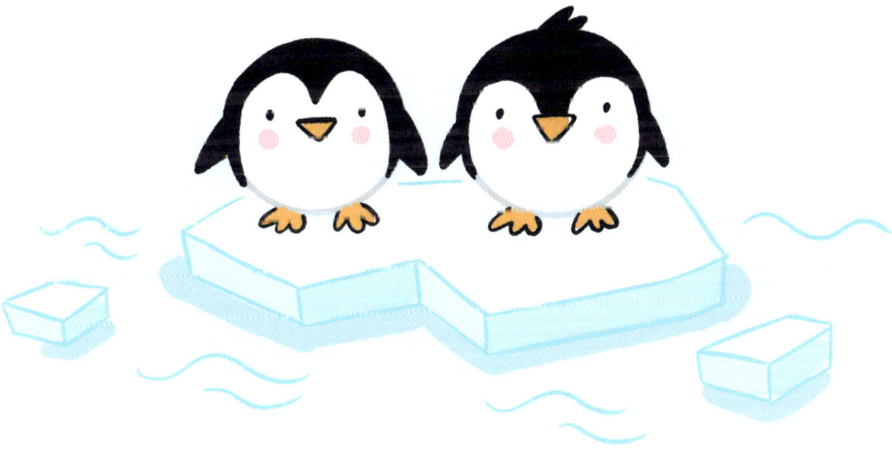

Koala

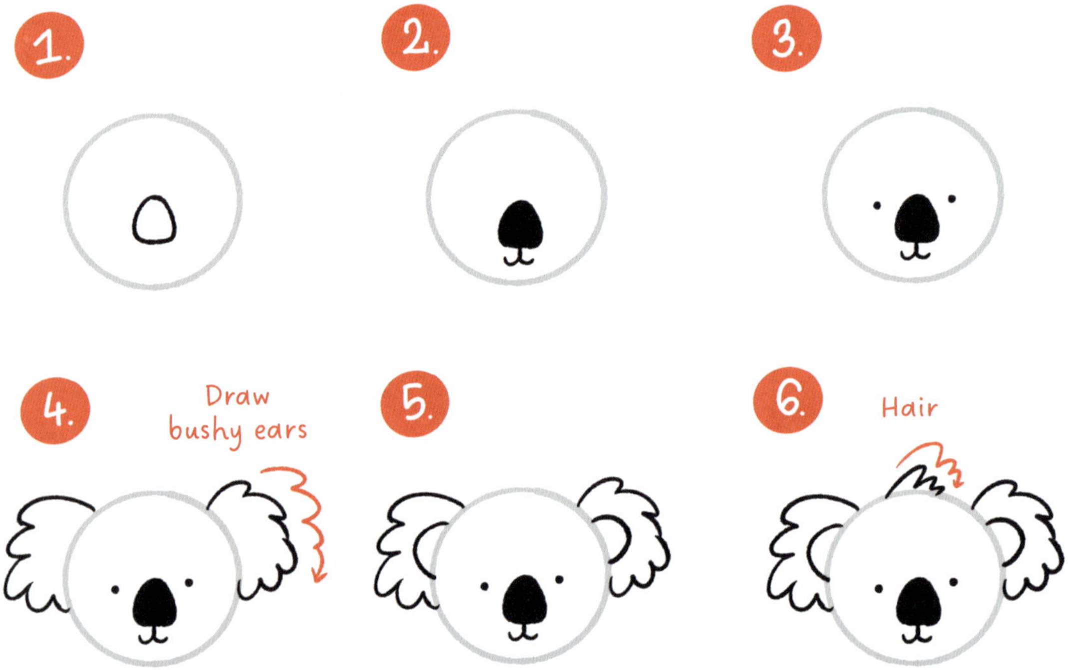
1.
2.
3.
4.
Draw bushy ears
5.
6.
Hair

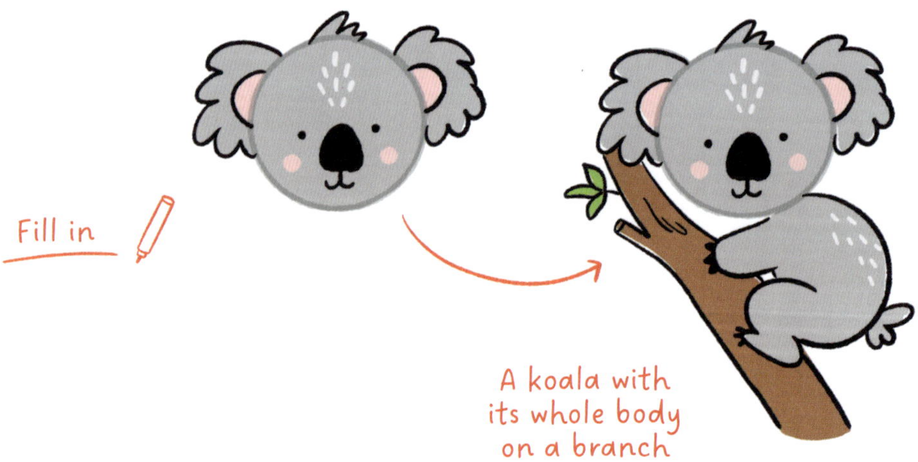
Fill in
A koala with its whole body on a branch

Sloth

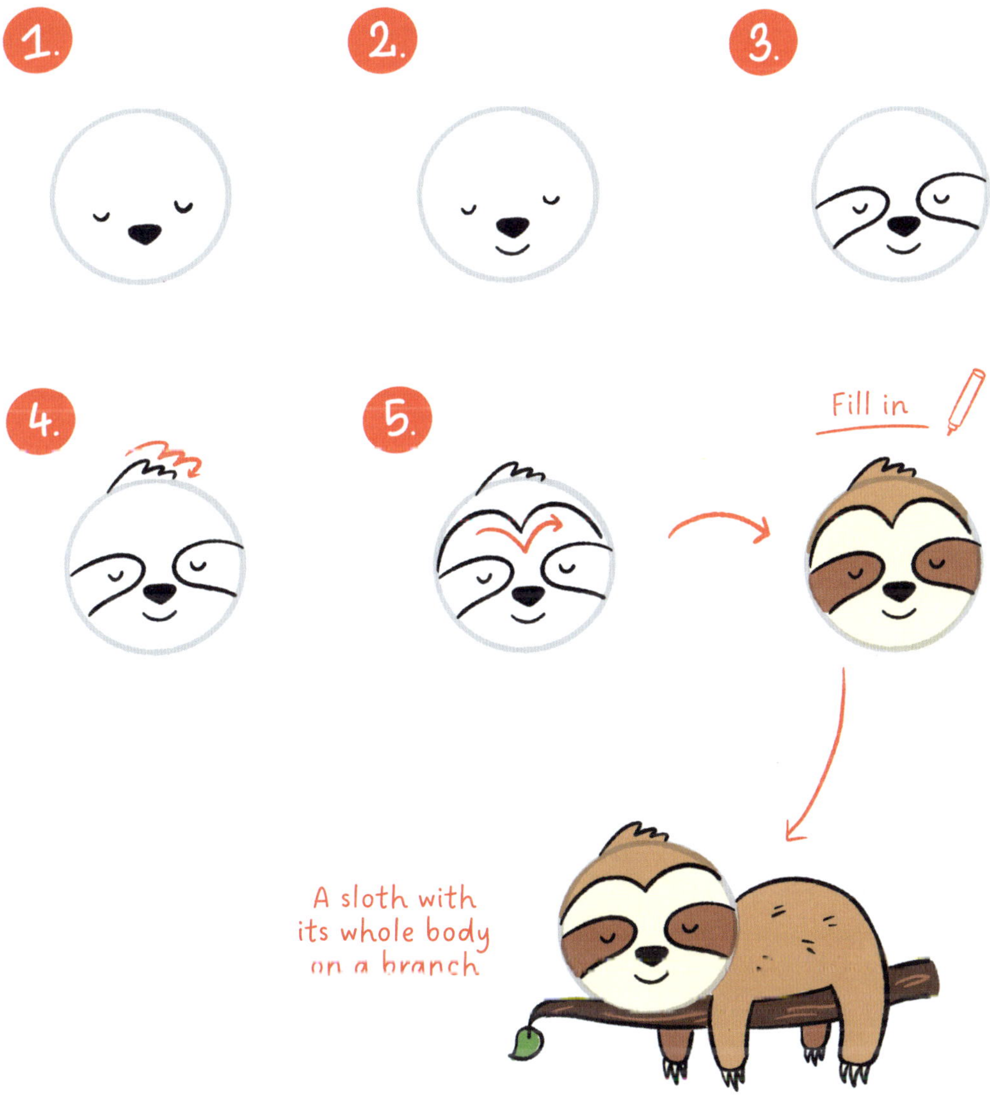

Panda

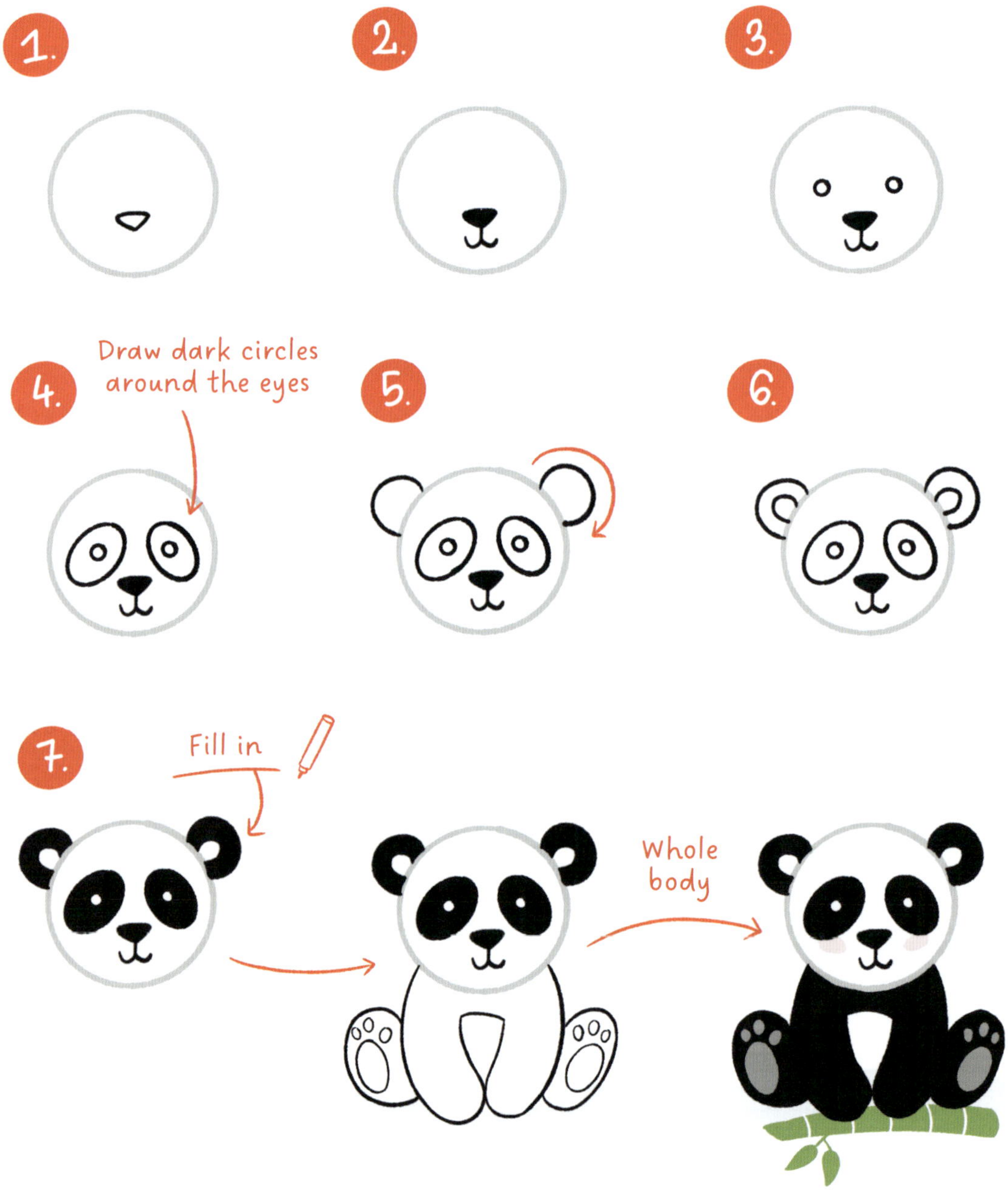

1.
2.
3.
4.
Draw dark circles around the eyes
5.
6.
7.
Fill in
Whole body

Beaver

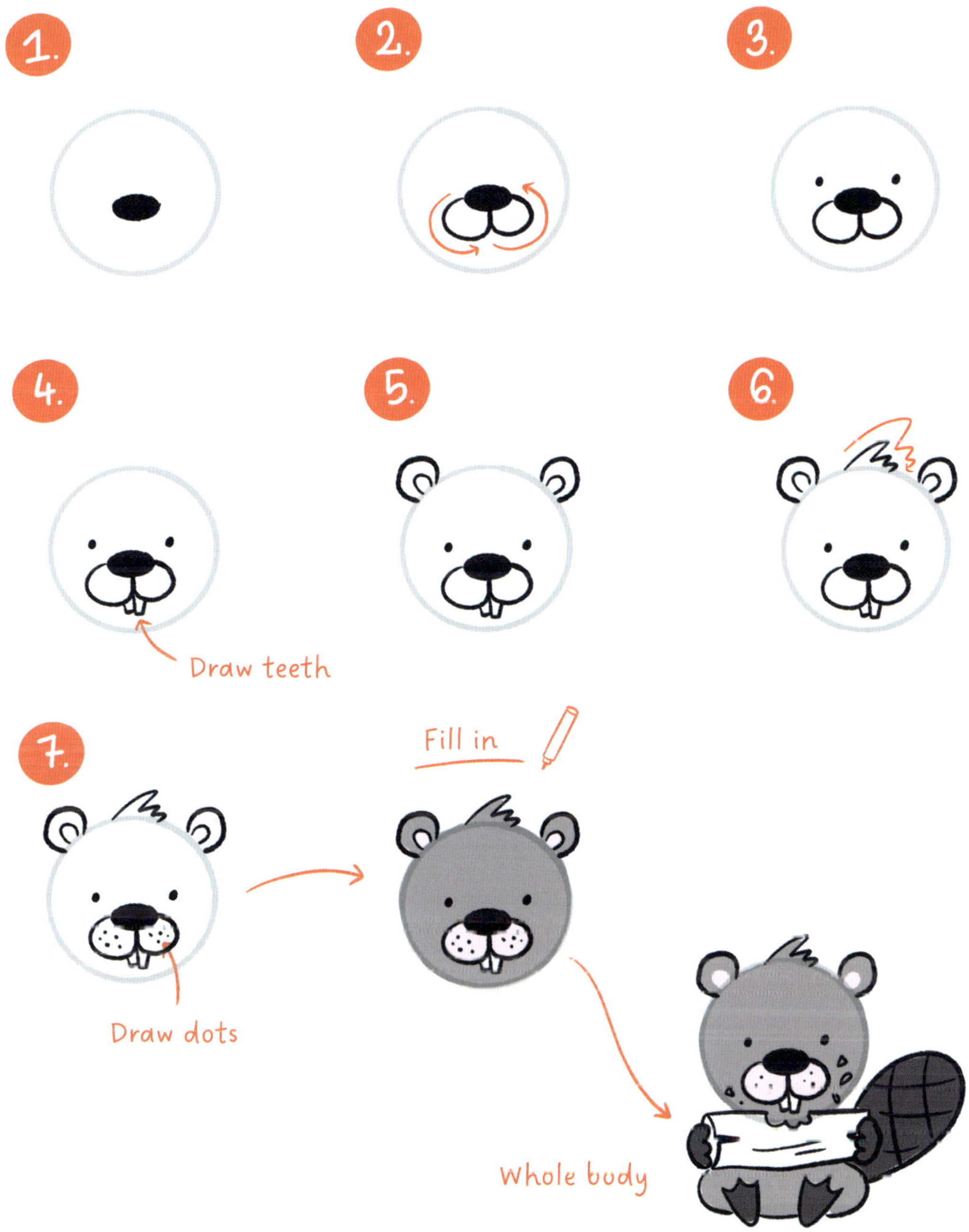

Donkey

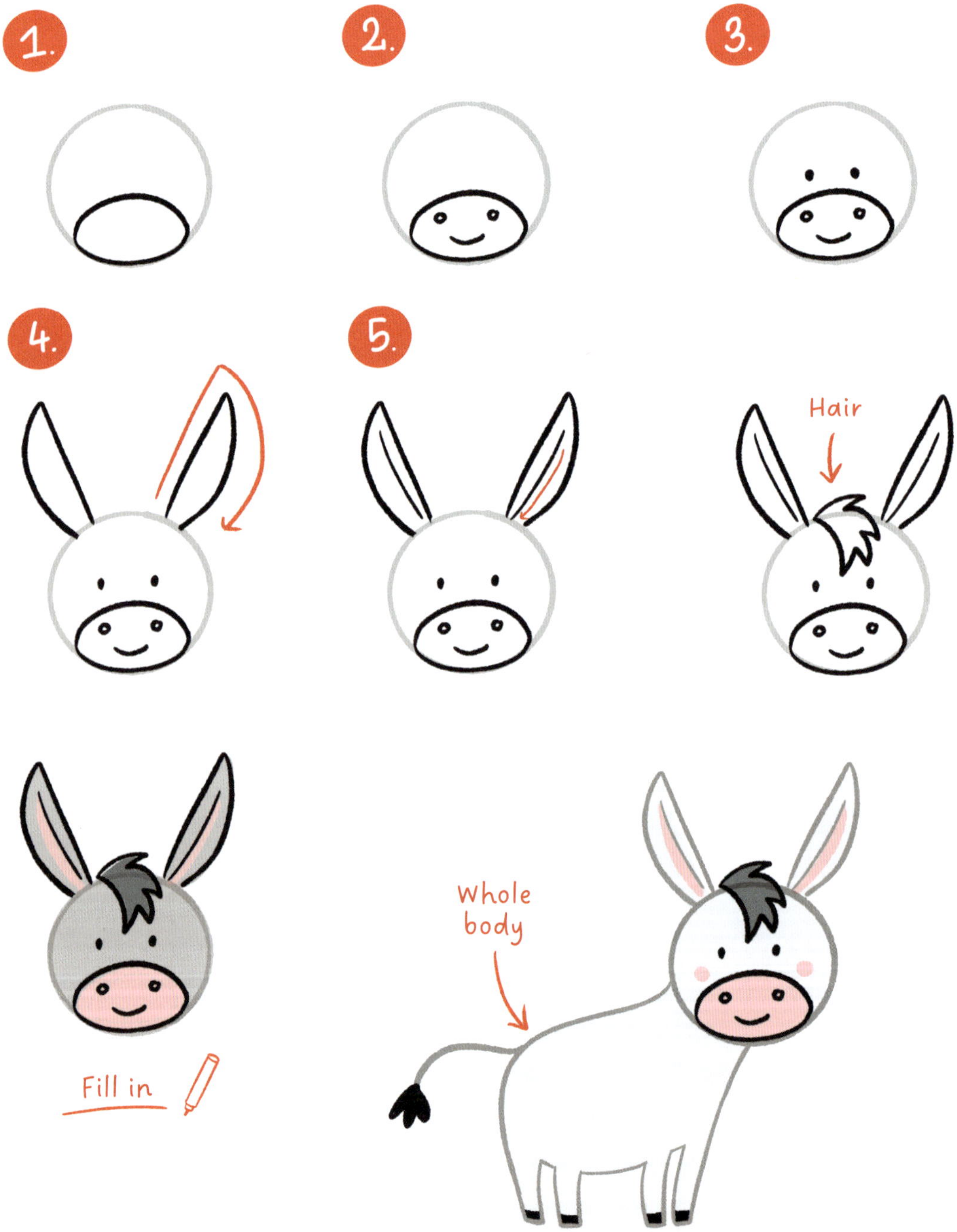

Rabbit

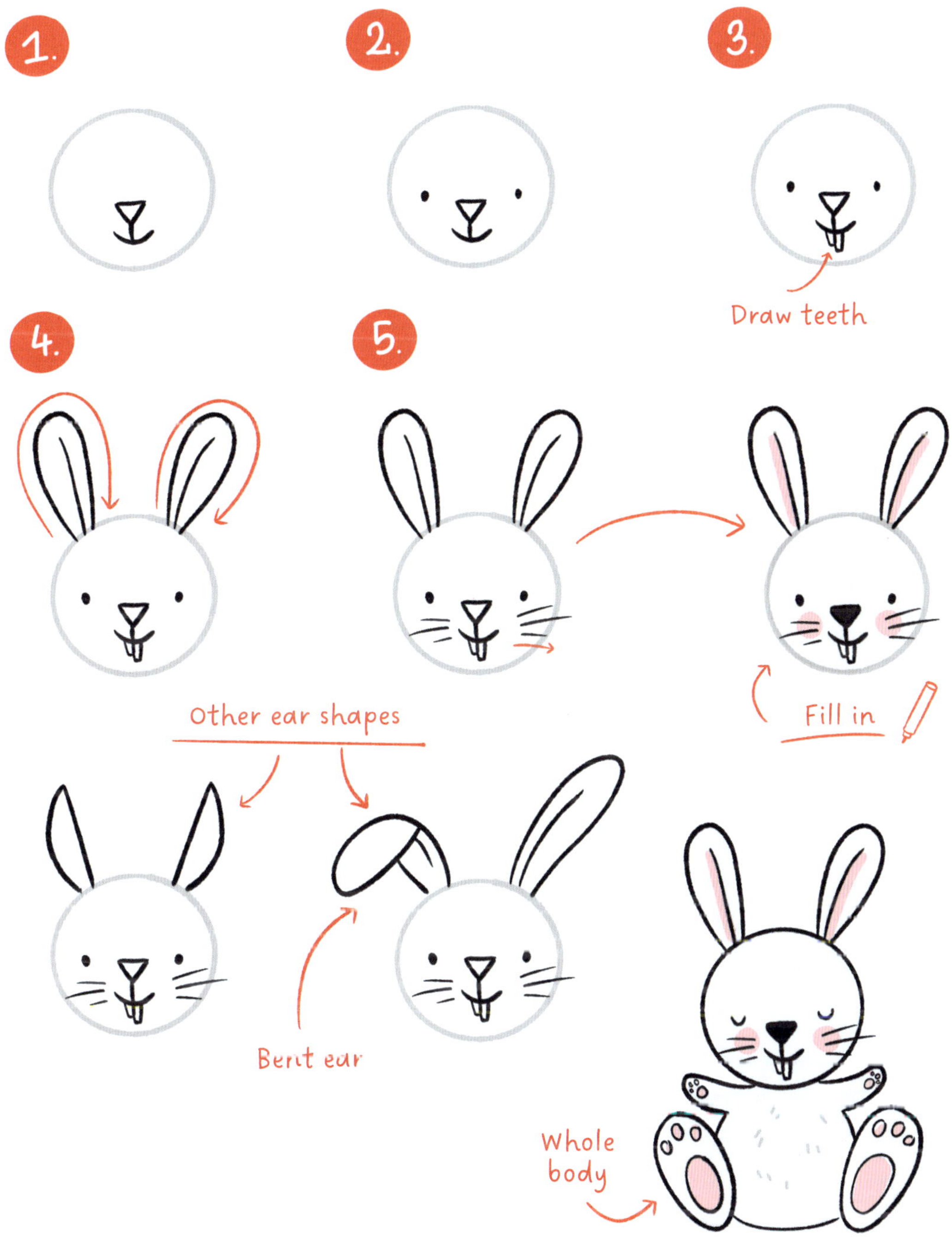
1.
2.
3.
Draw teeth
4.
5.
Fill in
Other ear shapes
Bent ear
Whole body

Goat

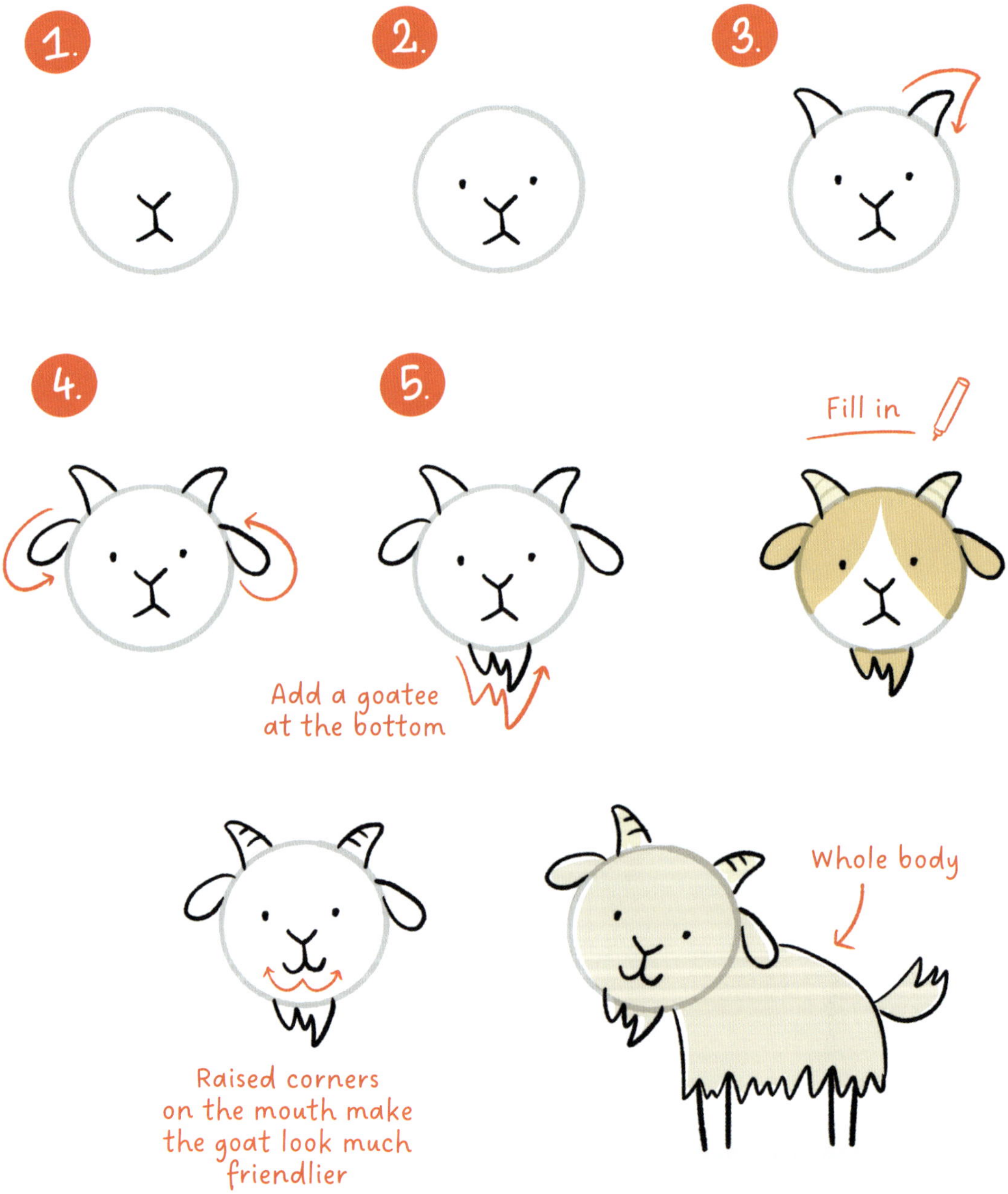
1.
2.
3.
4.
5.
Fill in
Add a goatee at the bottom
Raised corners on the mouth make the goat look much friendlier
Whole body

Sheep

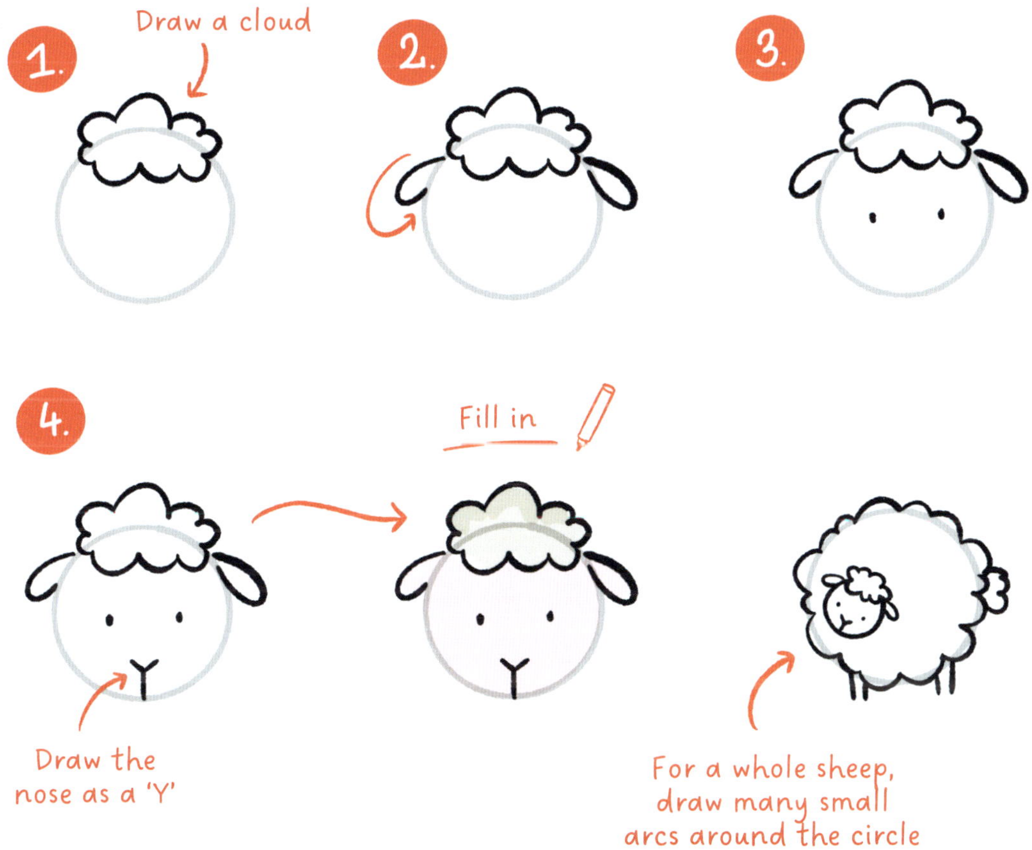
1.
Draw a cloud
2.
3.
4.
Fill in
Draw the nose as a 'Y'
For a whole sheep, draw many small arcs around the circle

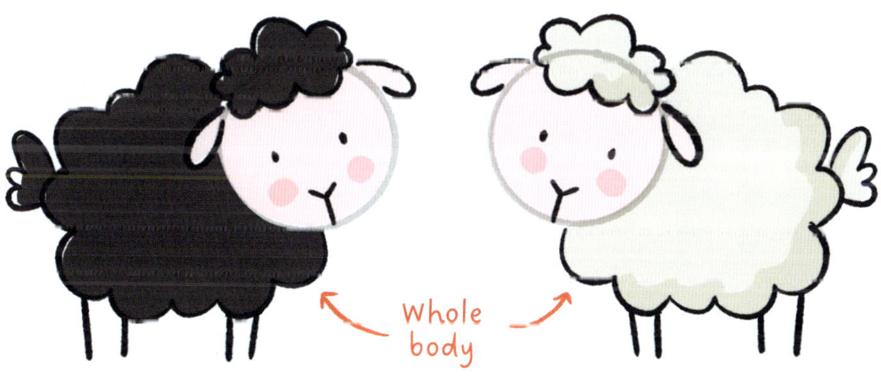
Whole body

Hedgehog

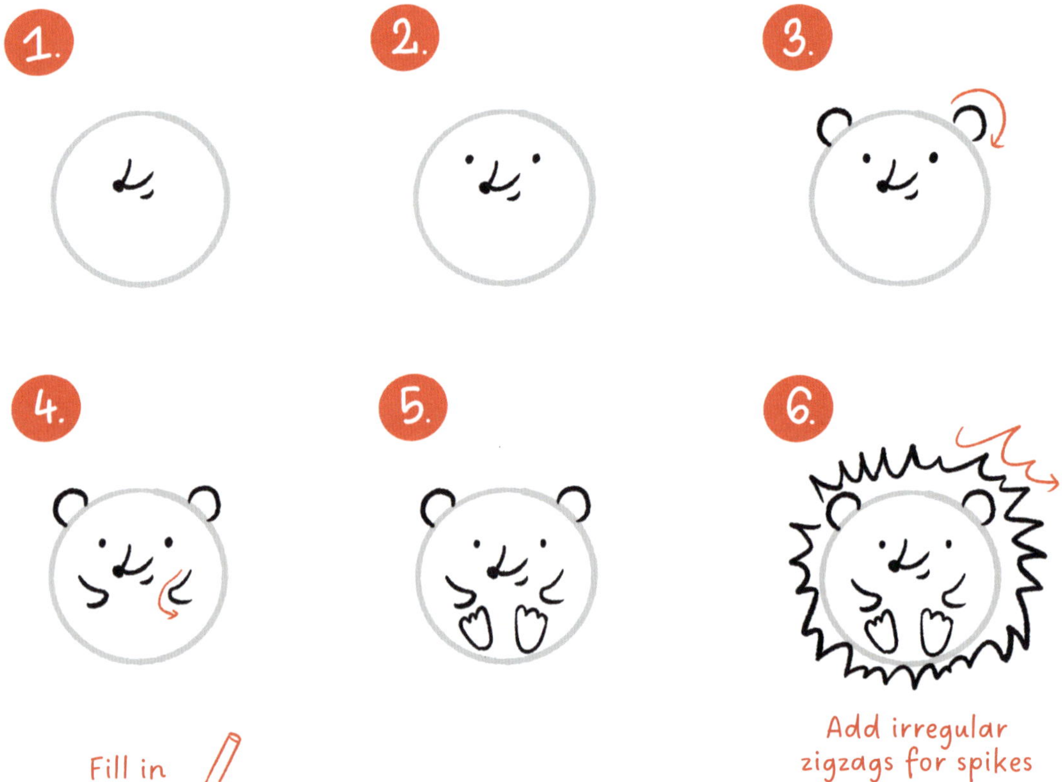
1.
2.
3.
4.
5.
6.
Add irregular zigzags for spikes

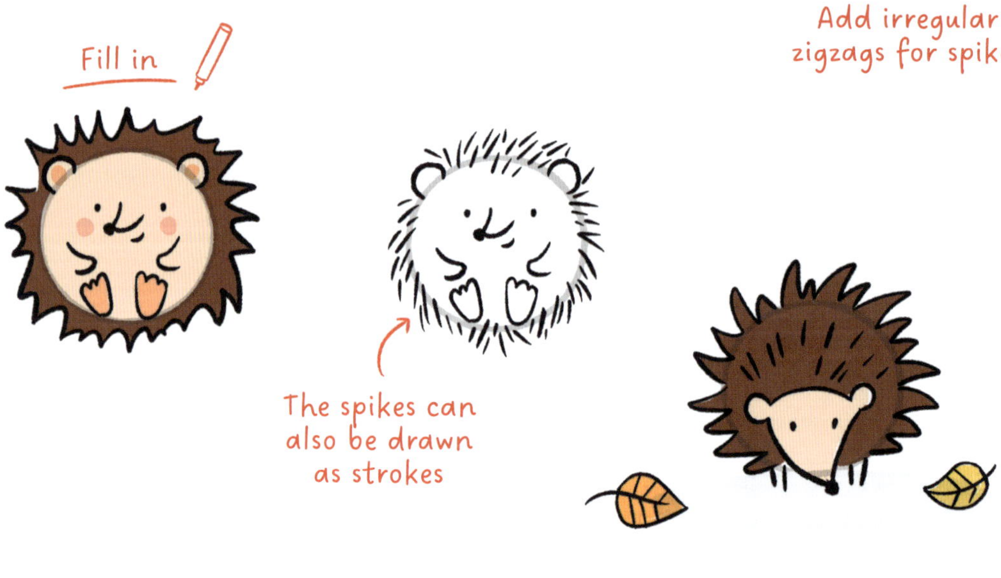
Fill in
The spikes can also be drawn as strokes

Deer

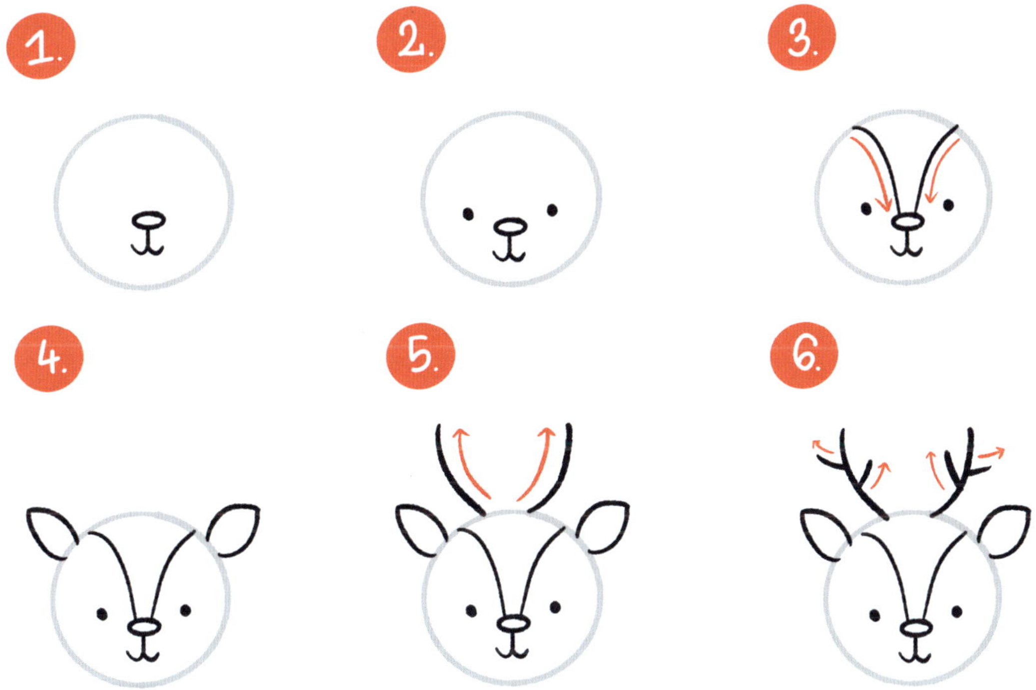

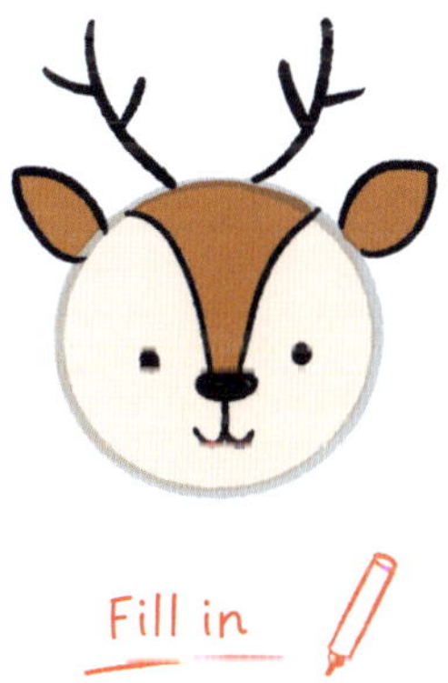

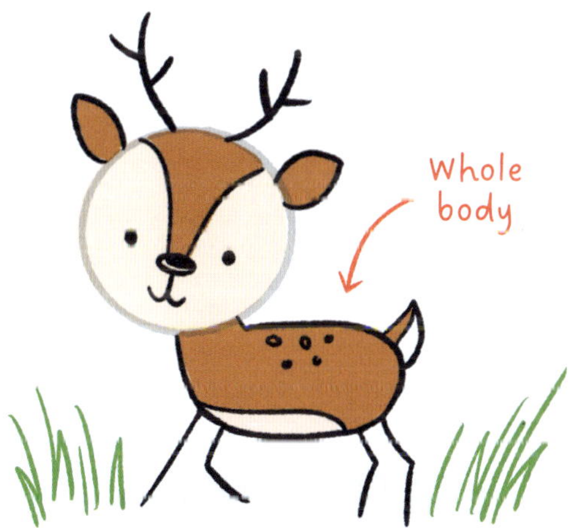

Ladybug

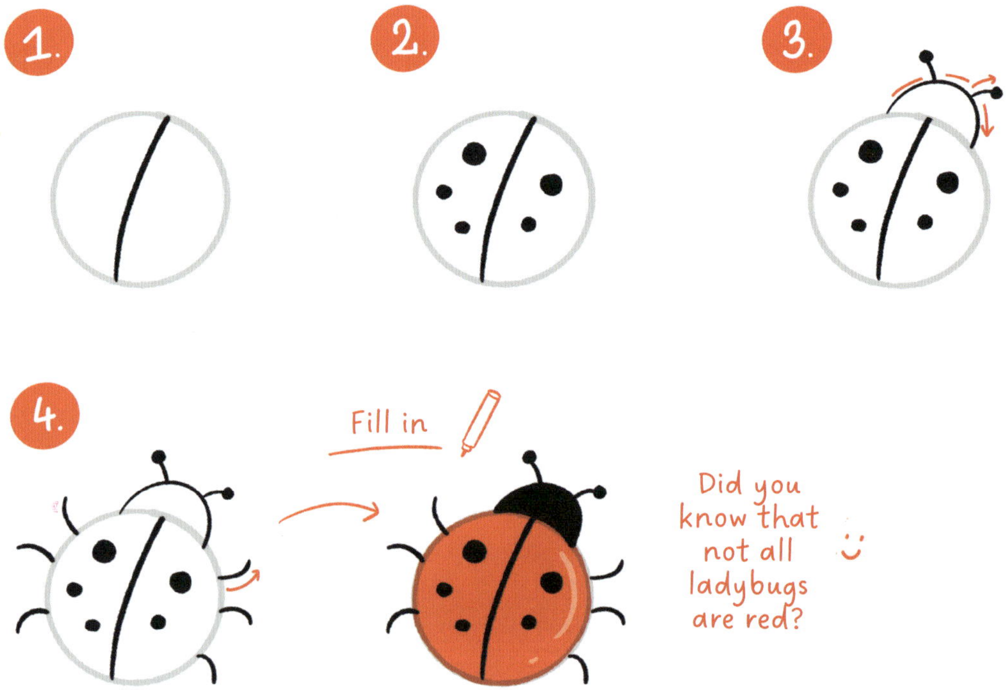
1.
2.
3.
4.
Fill in
Did you know that not all ladybugs are red?

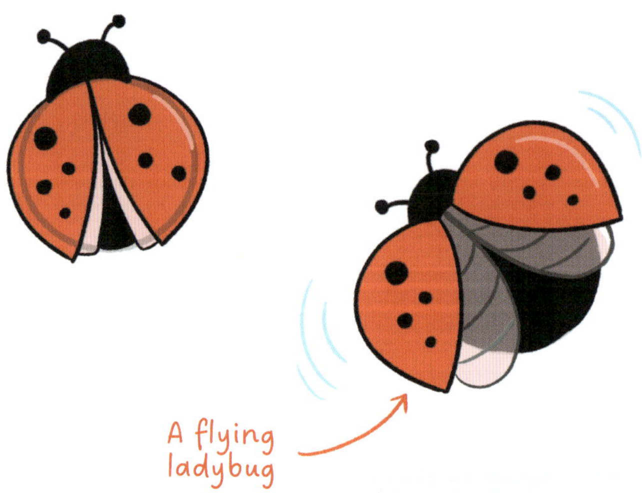
A flying ladybug

Monkey

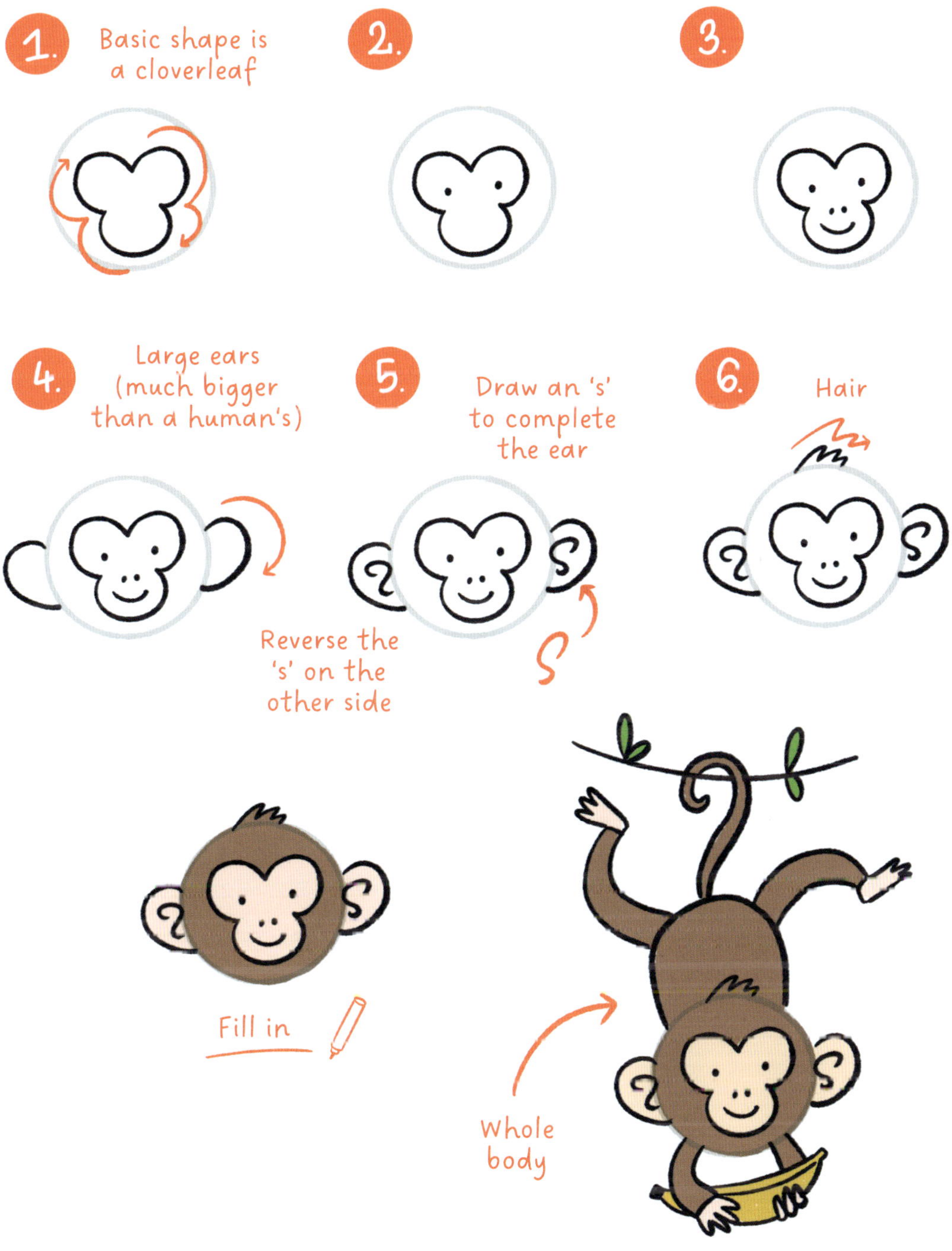
1.
Basic shape is a cloverleaf
2.
3.
4.
Large ears (much bigger than a human's)
5.
Draw an 's' to complete the ear
Reverse the 's' on the other side
6.
Hair
Fill in
Whole body

Lion

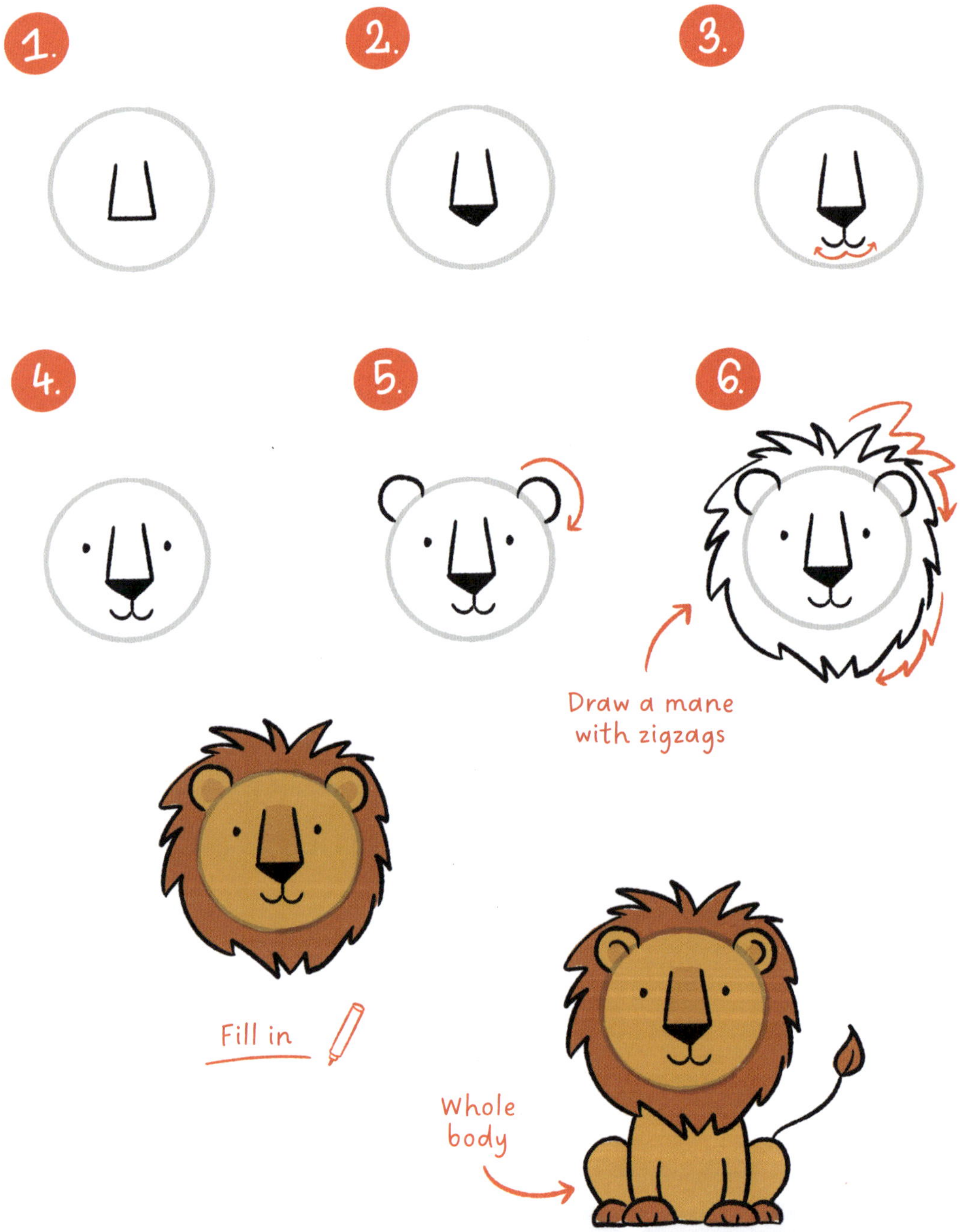

Tiger

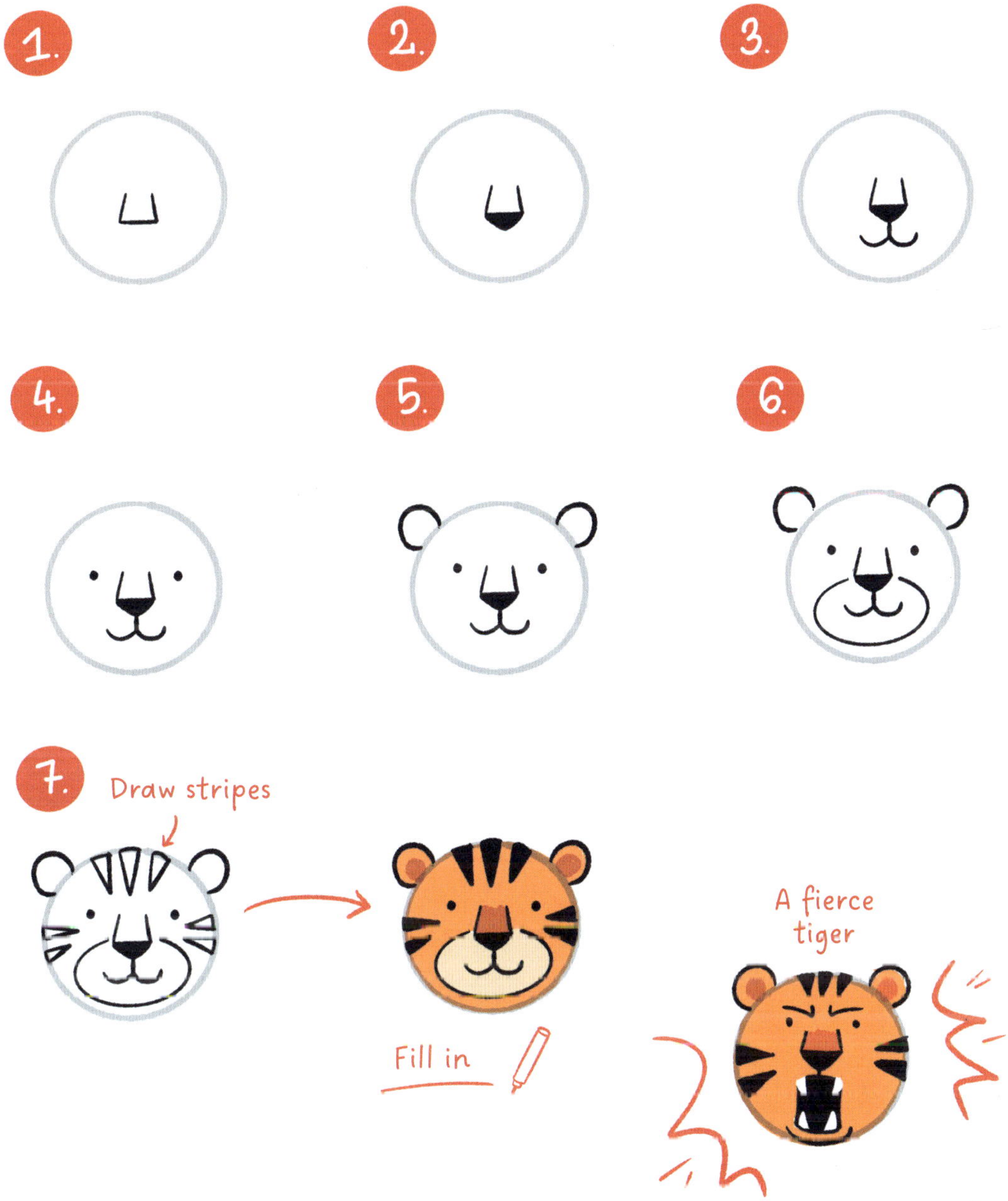

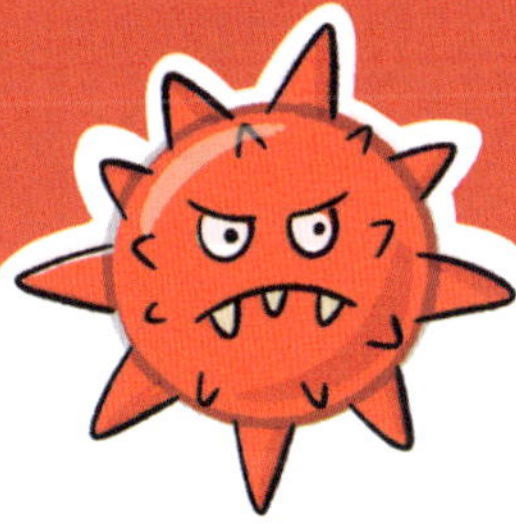

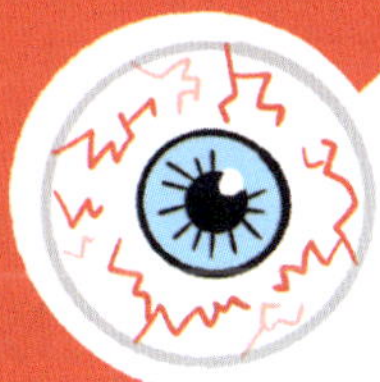

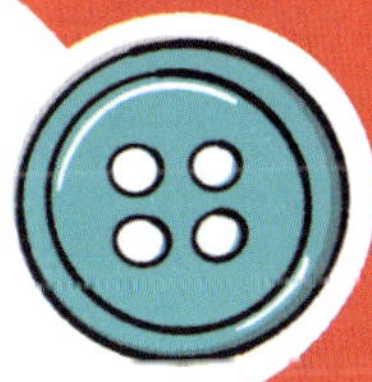

CHAPTER 2

Things

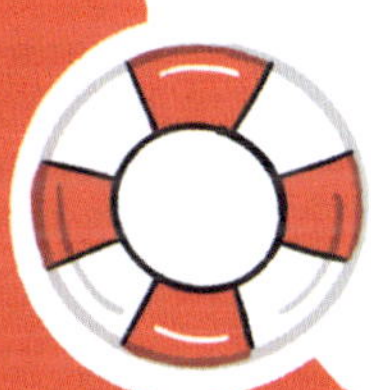

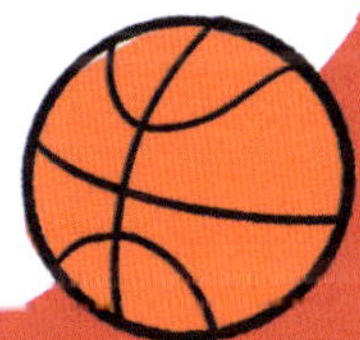

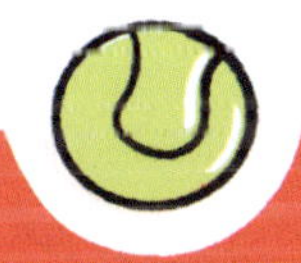

Button

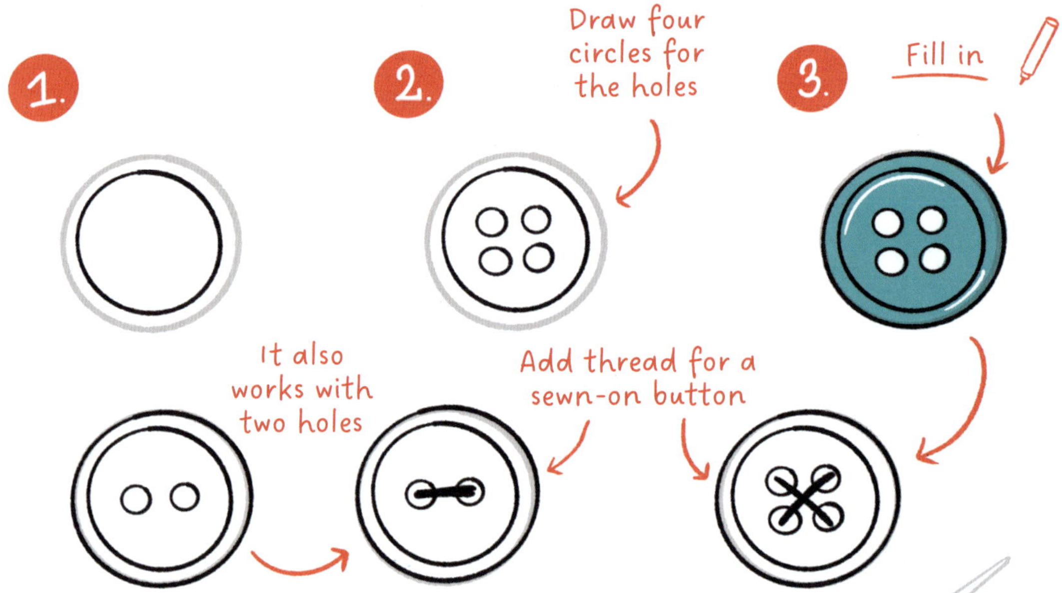

Ball of wool

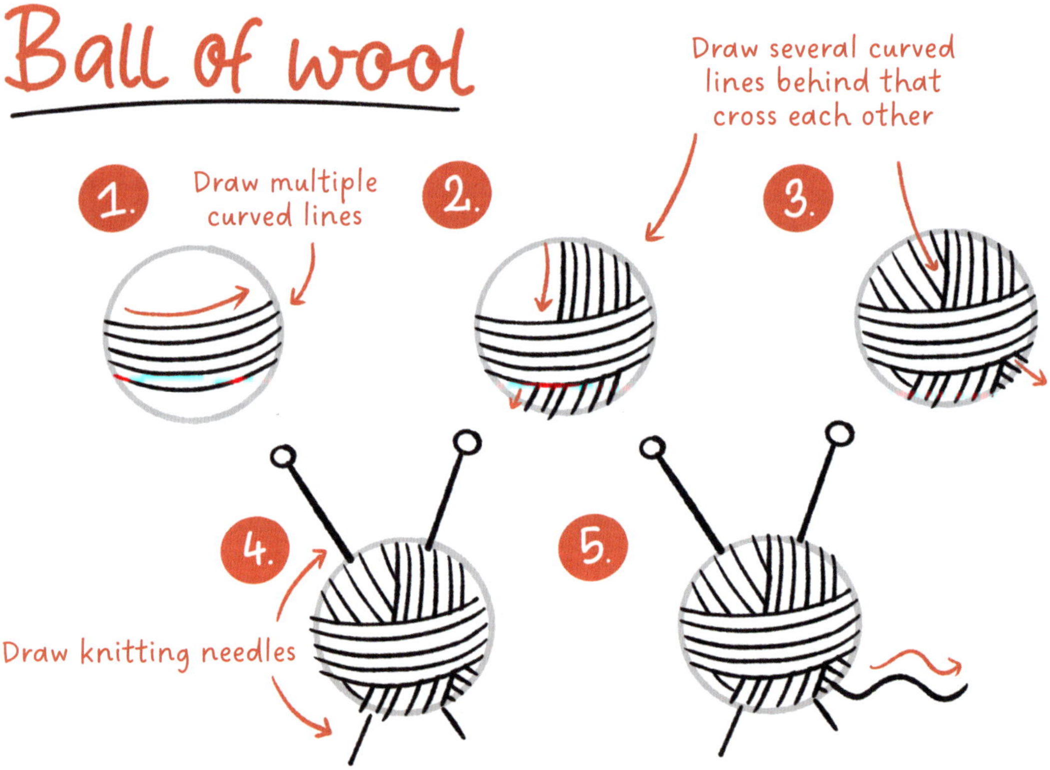

Clock

1.

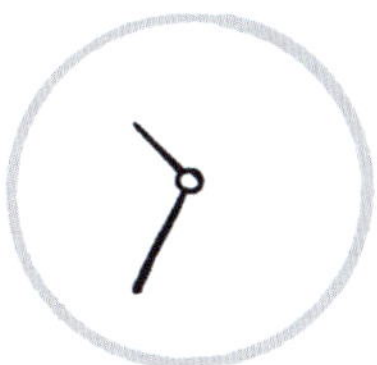

2.

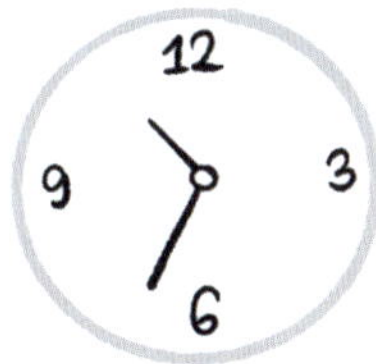

3.

4.

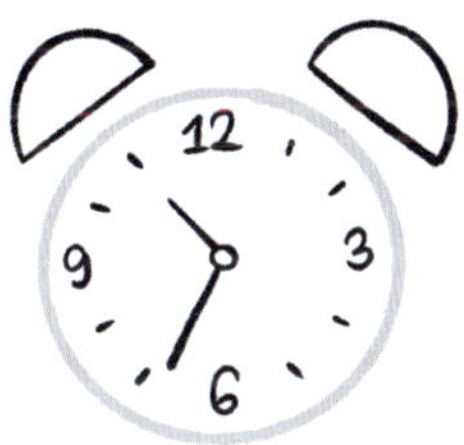

5.

Draw details

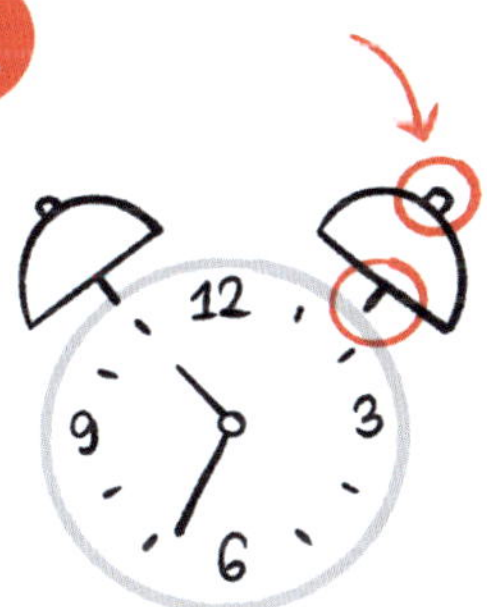

6.

7.

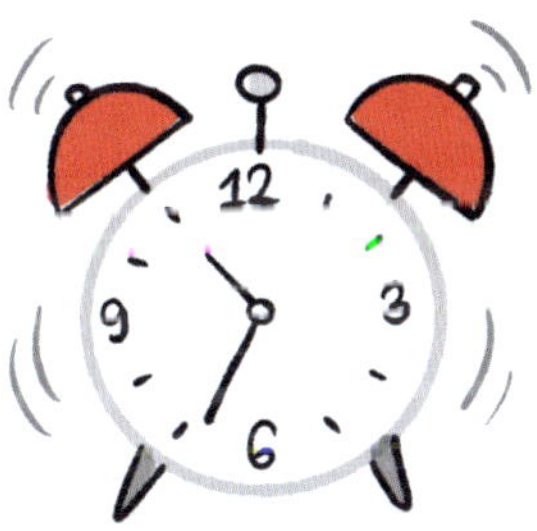

Other clocks

Wall clock

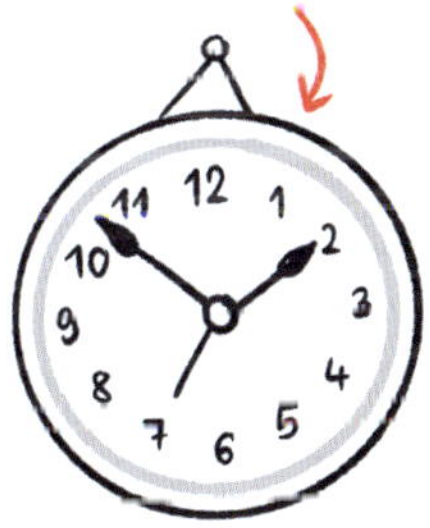

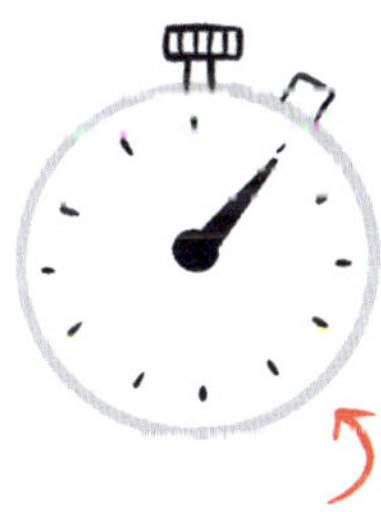

Stopwatch

Wristwatch

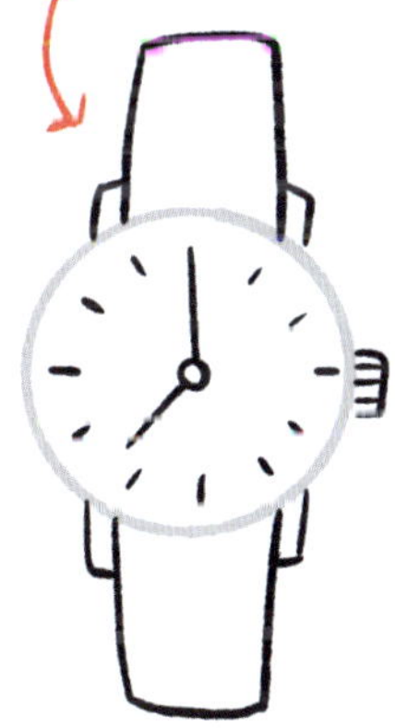

Ball

Basketball

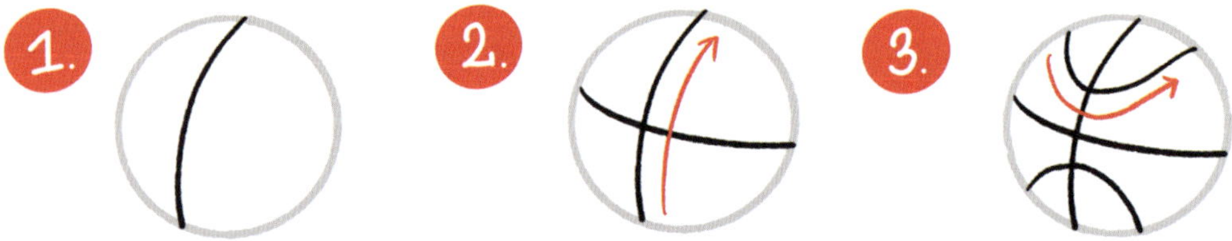

Football

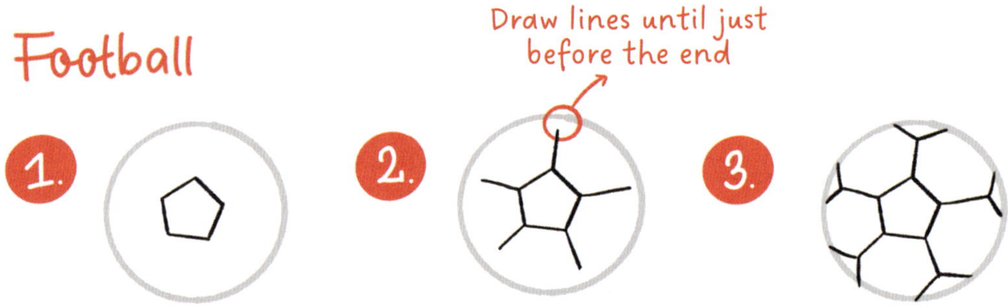

Volleyball

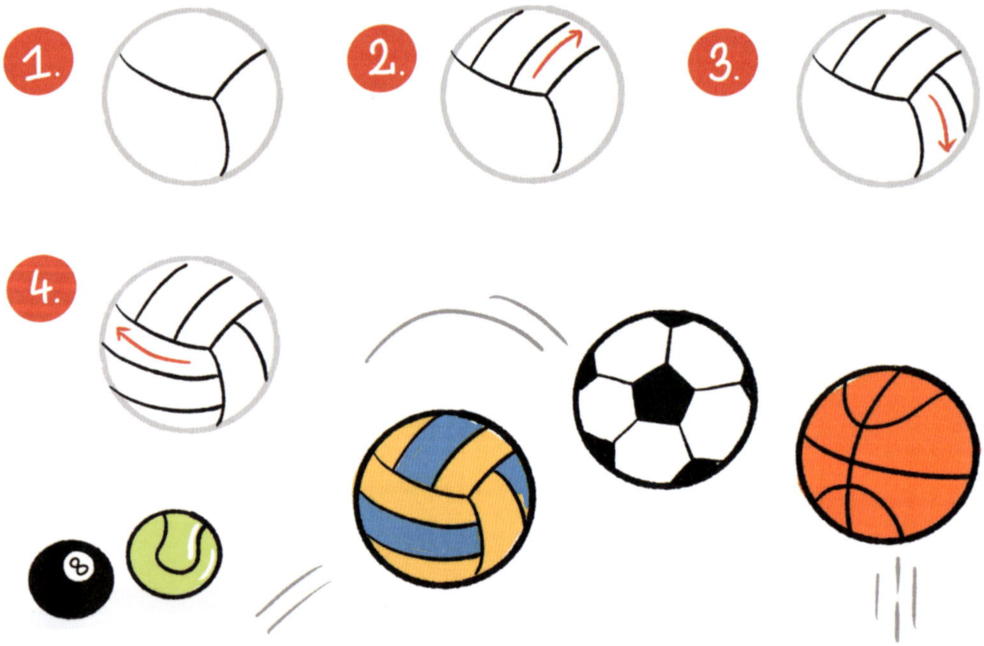

Life ring

1.

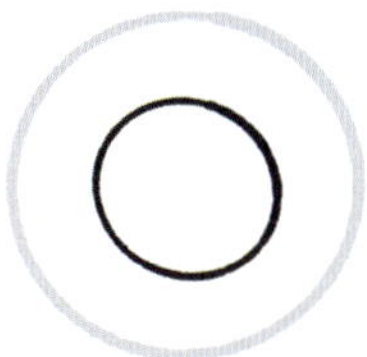

2.

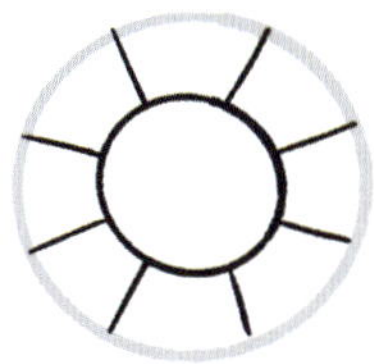

3.

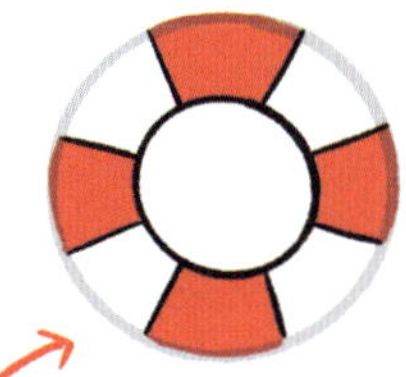

It is important to fill in every second segment

4.

Use white and grey lines to indicate reflections and shadows

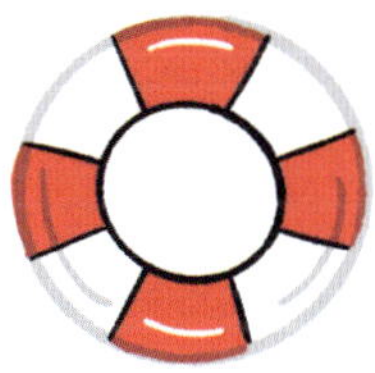

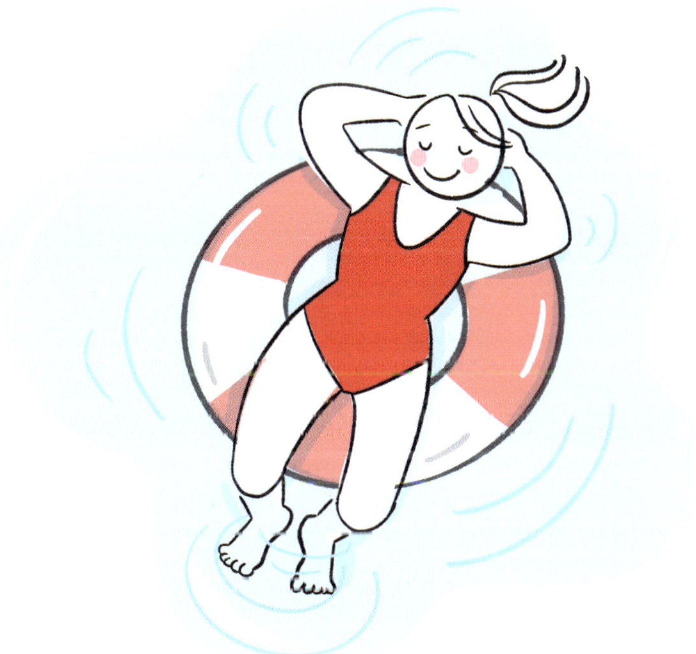

Cactus

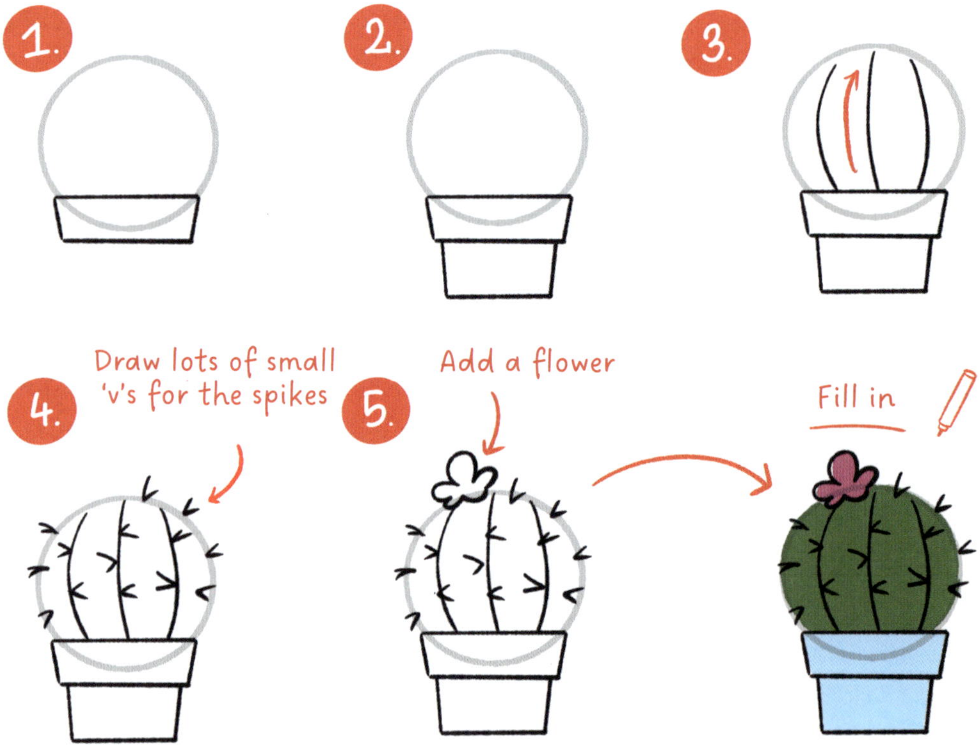
1.
2.
3.
4.
Draw lots of small 'v's for the spikes
5.
Add a flower
Fill in

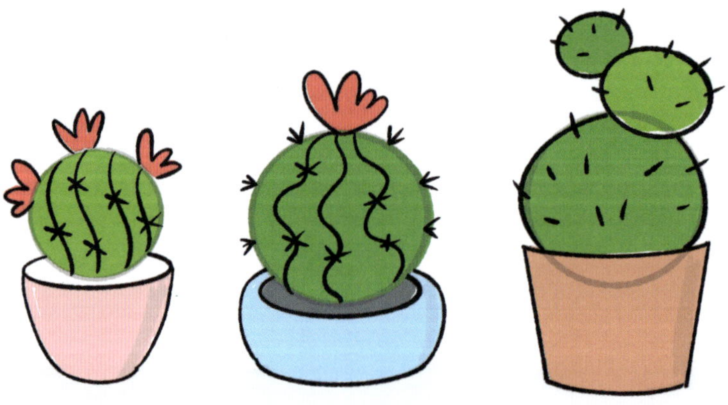

Flower

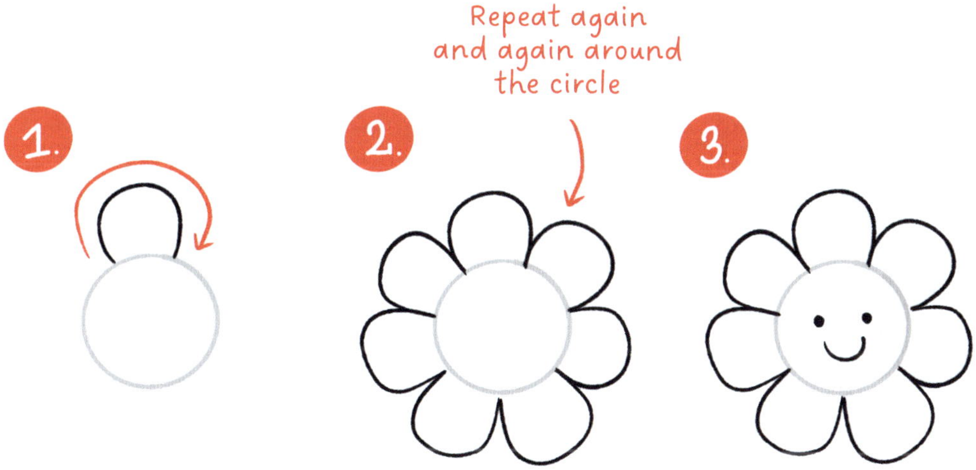
1.
2.
3.
Repeat again and again around the circle

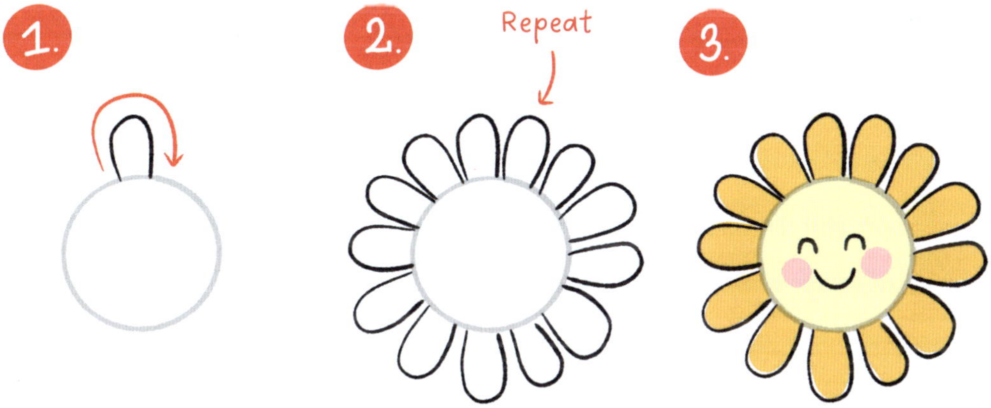
1.
2.
3.
Repeat

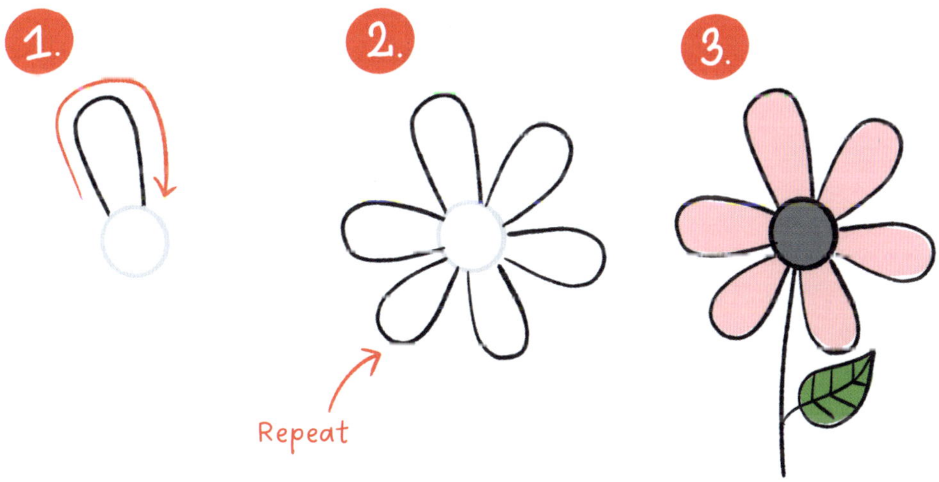
1.
2.
3.
Repeat

Tree

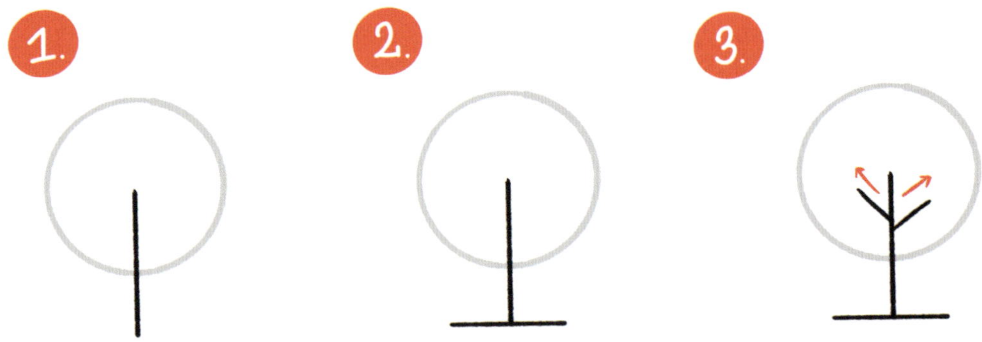

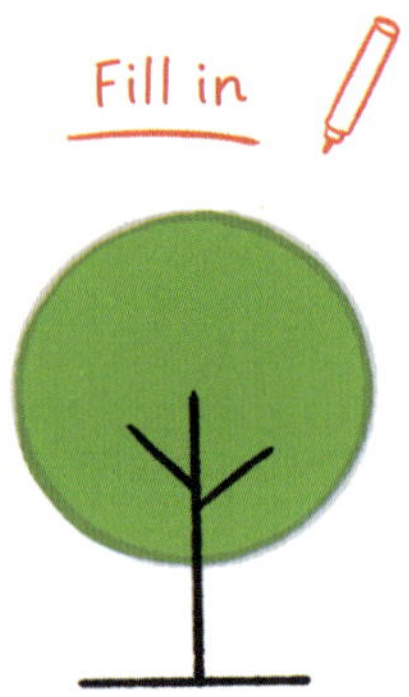

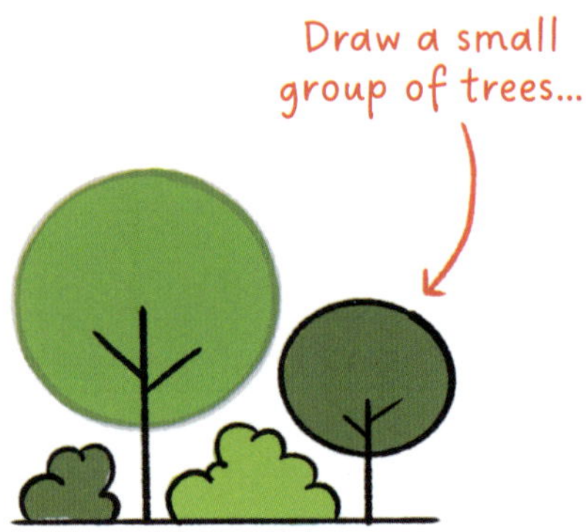

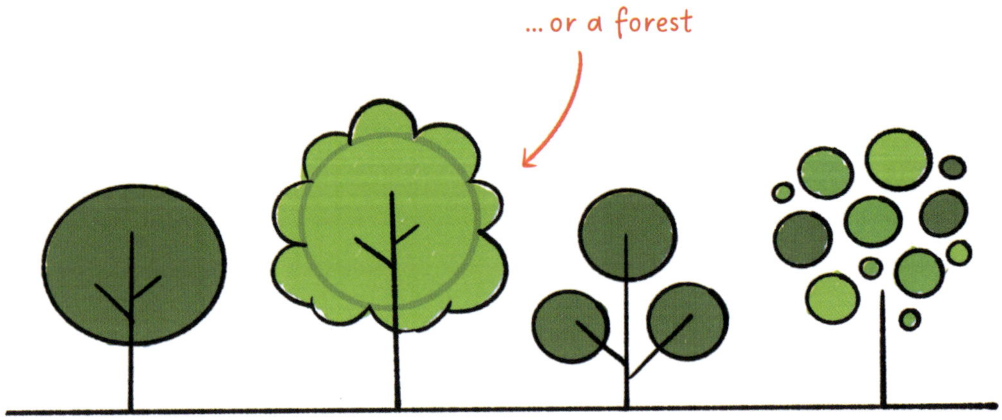

Planet

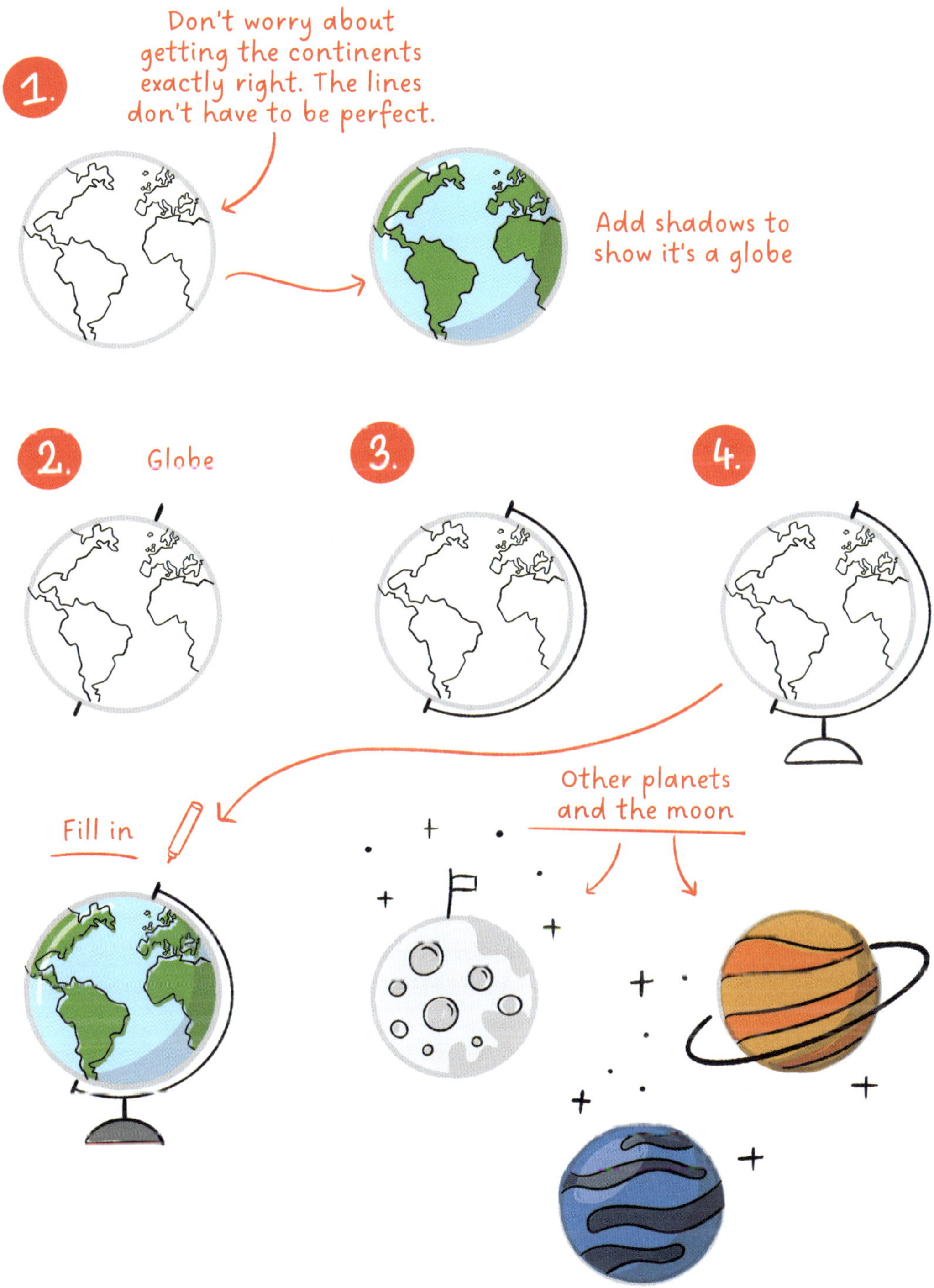
1.
Don't worry about getting the continents exactly right. The lines don't have to be perfect.
Add shadows to show it's a globe
2.
Globe
3.
4.
Fill in
Other planets and the moon

Sun

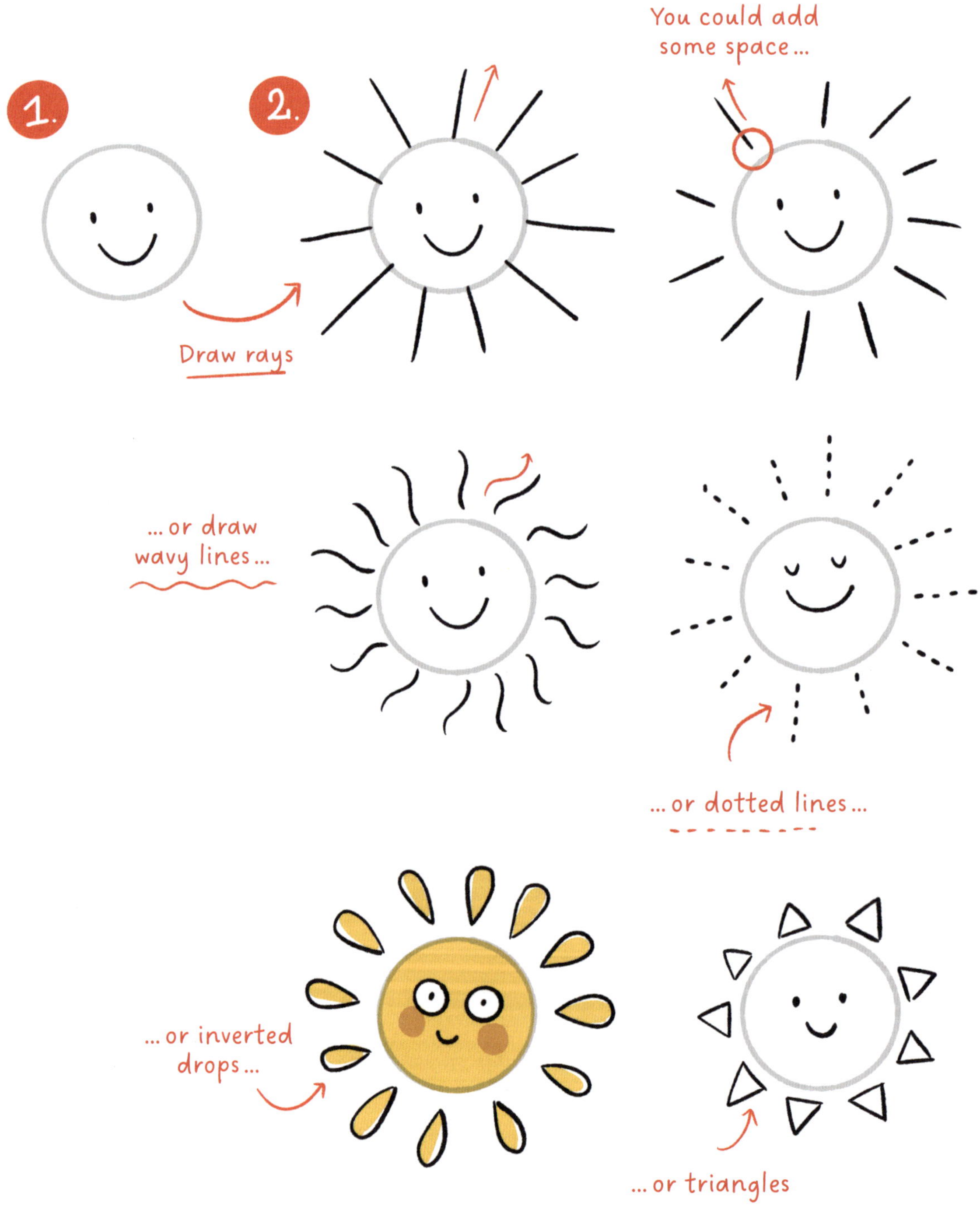
1.
2.
Draw rays
You could add some space...
... or draw wavy lines...
... or dotted lines...
... or inverted drops...
... or triangles

Snowman

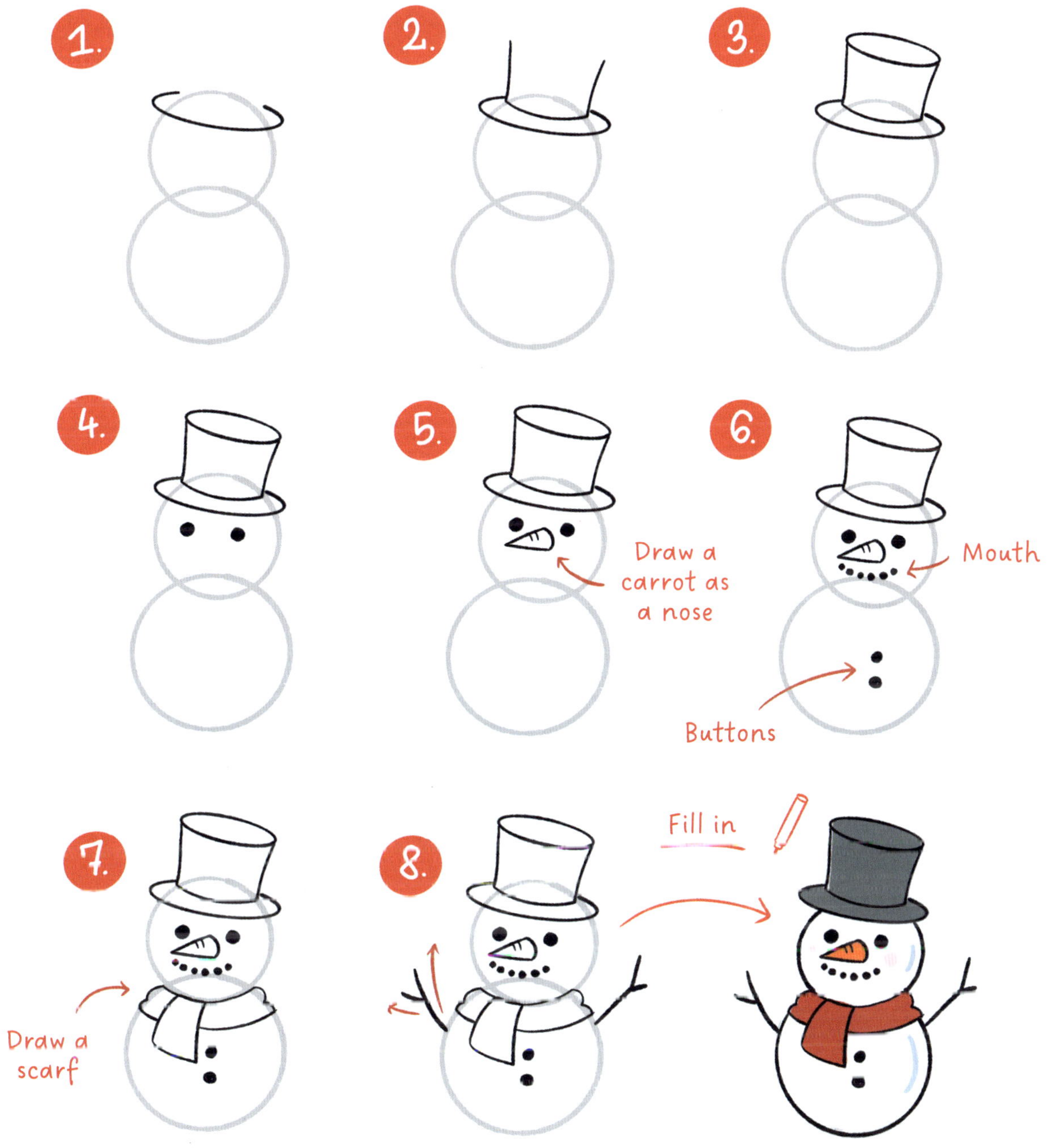
1.
2.
3.
4.
5.
Draw a carrot as a nose
6.
Mouth
Buttons
7.
Draw a scarf
8.
Fill in

Bicycle

1.

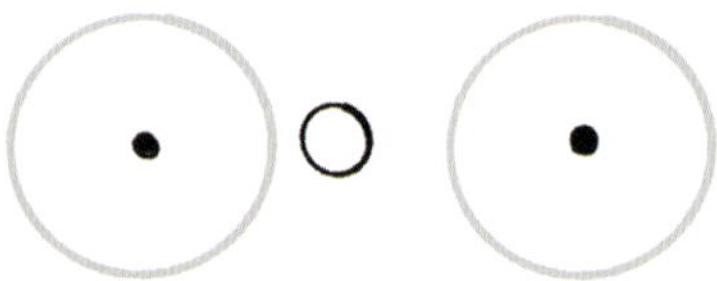

2.

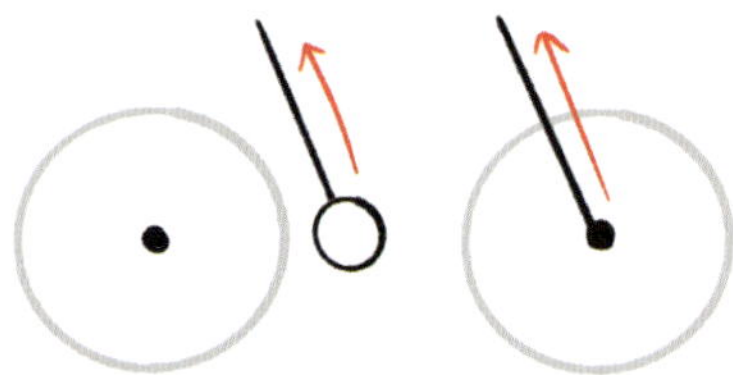

3.

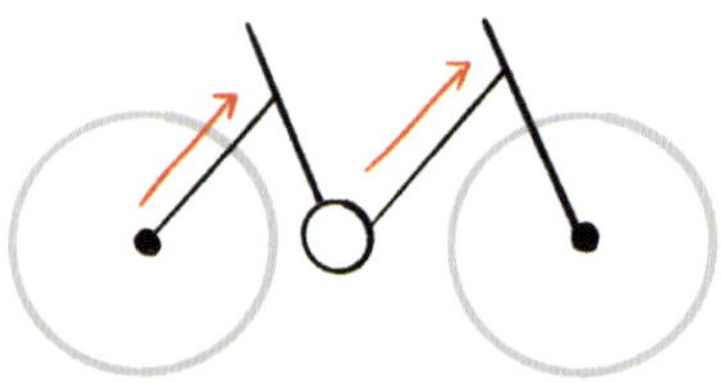

4.

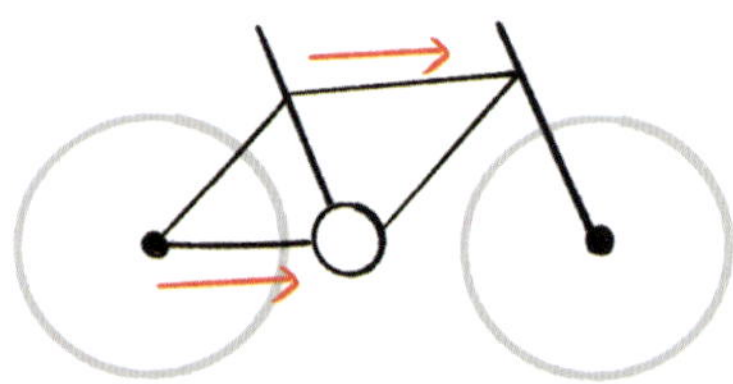

5.

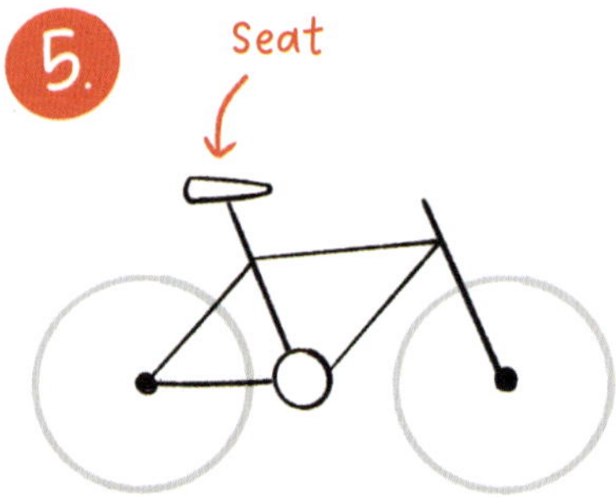

6.

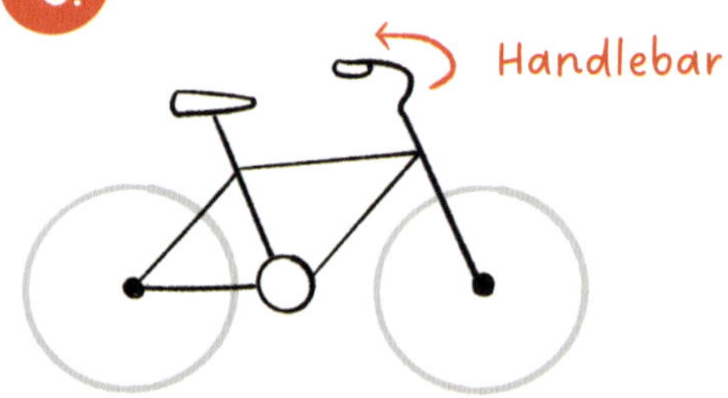

7.

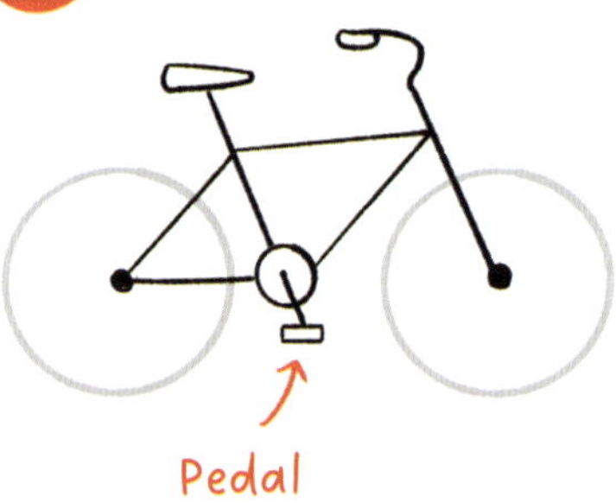

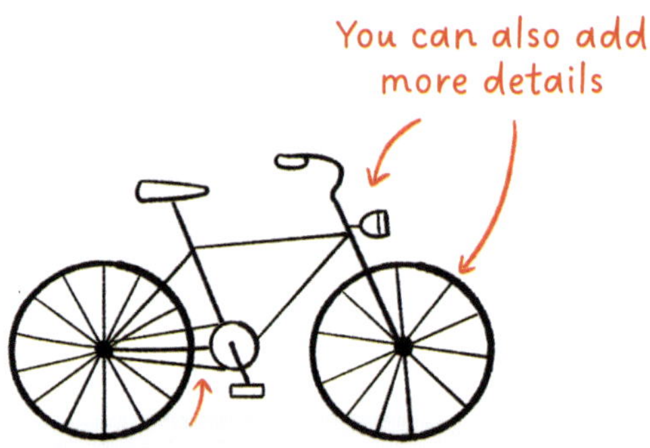

Wheelchair

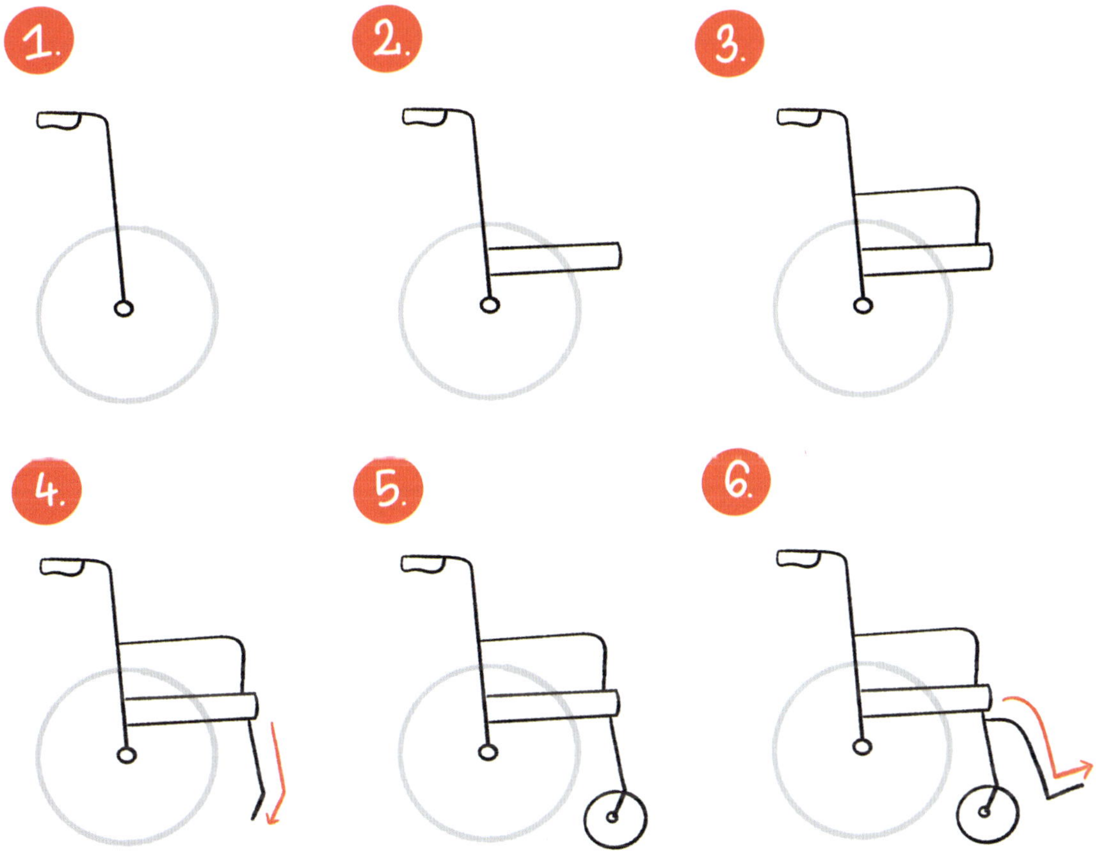

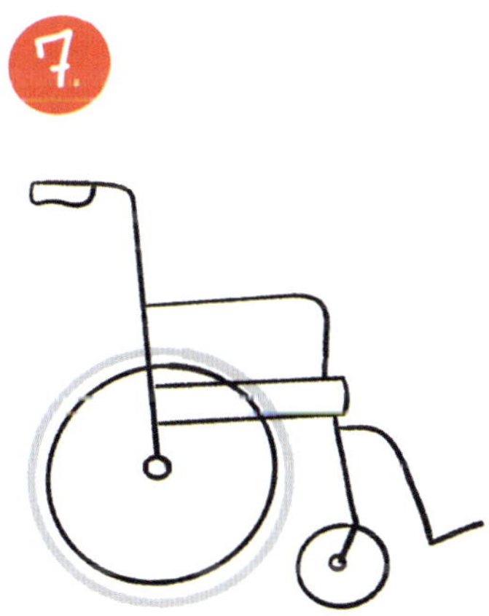

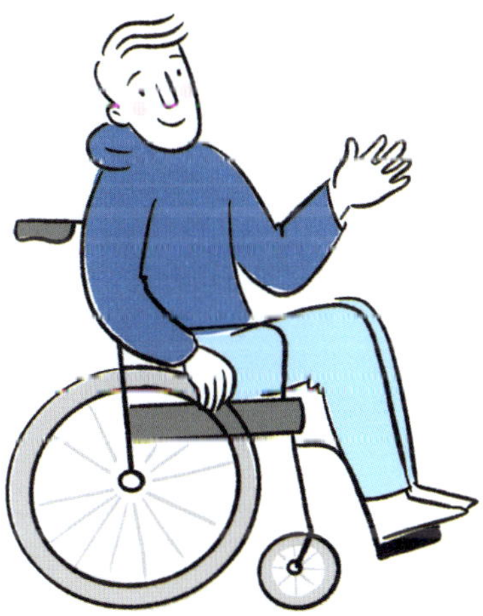

Germ

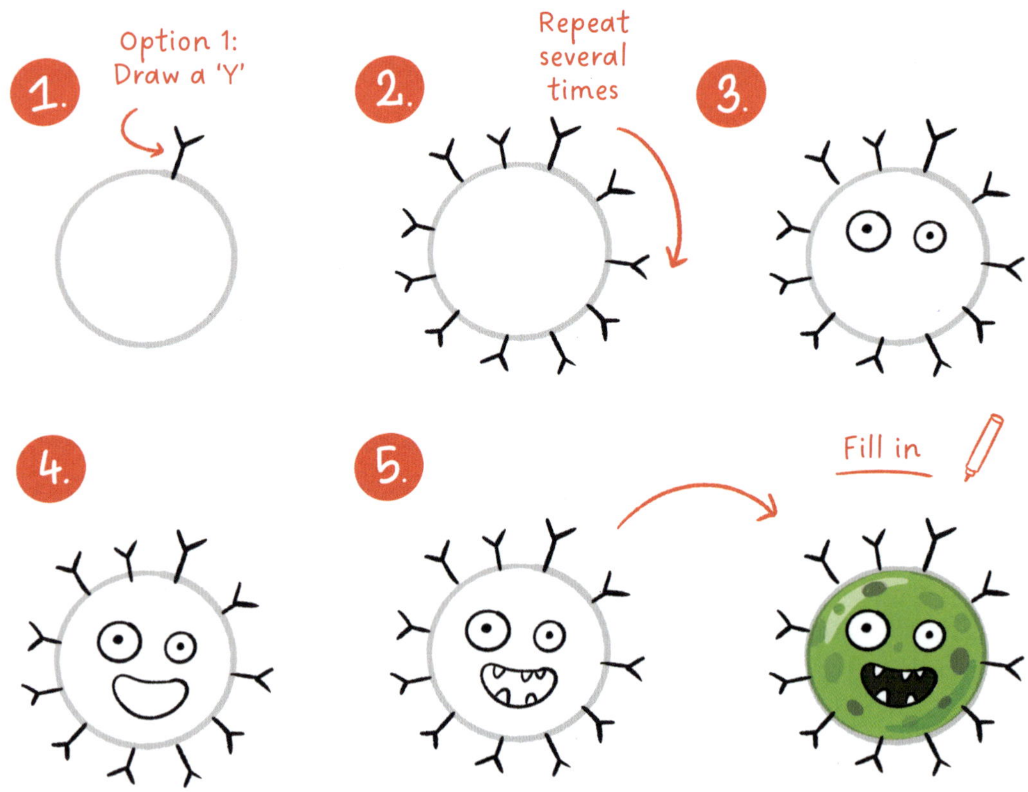
1.
Option 1: Draw a 'Y'
2.
Repeat several times
3.
4.
5.
Fill in

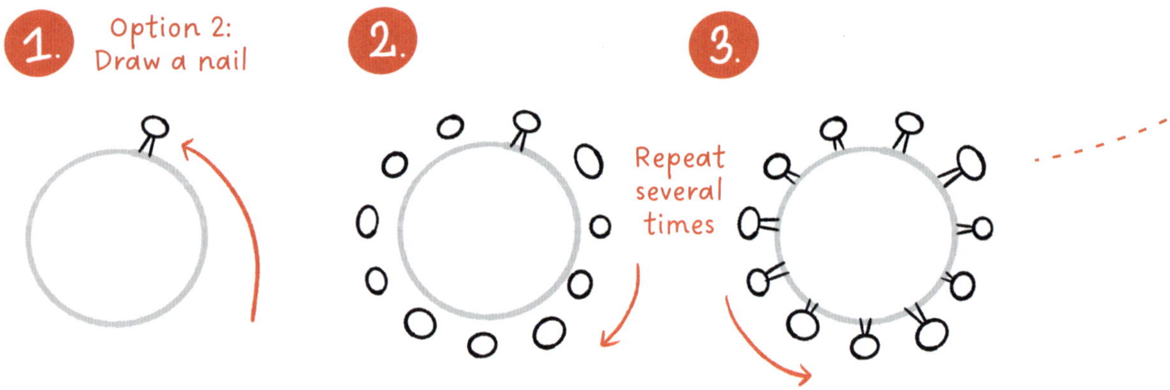
1.
Option 2: Draw a nail
2.
Repeat several times
3.

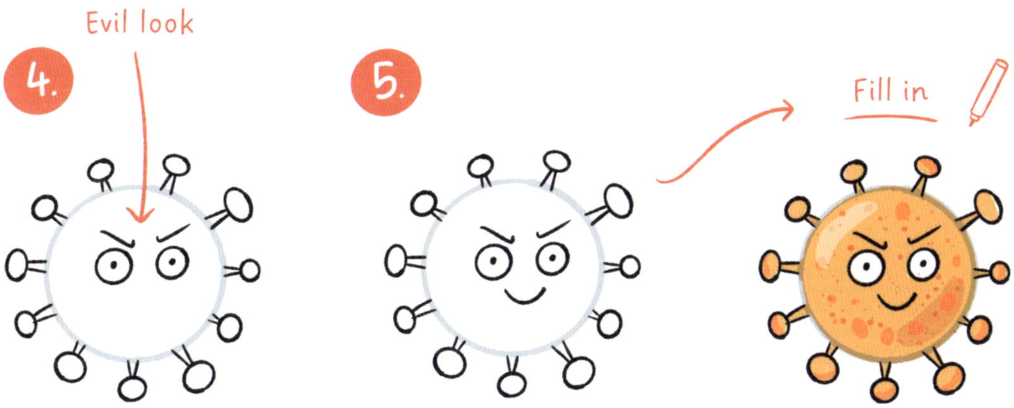
Evil look
4.
5.
Fill in

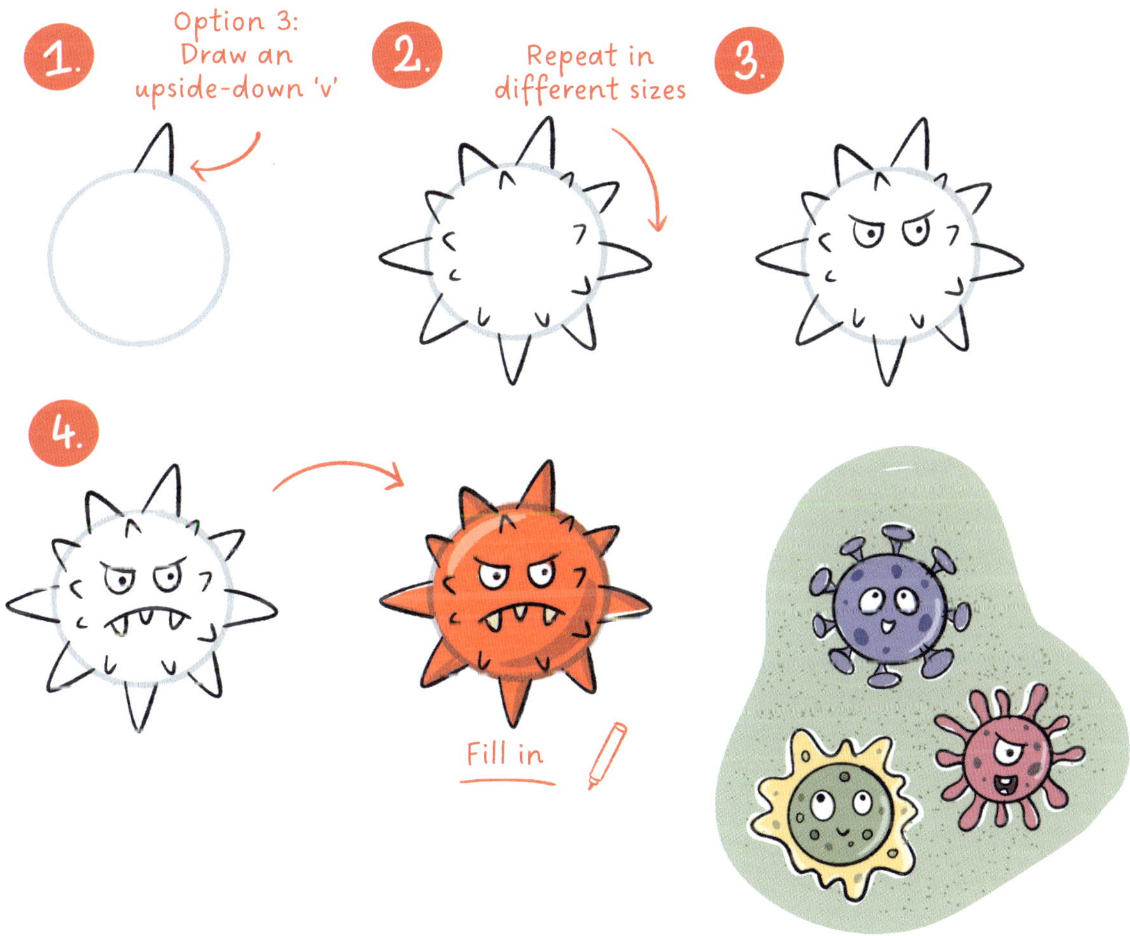
1.
Option 3:
Draw an
upside-down 'v'
2.
Repeat in
different sizes
3.
4.
Fill in

Eyeball

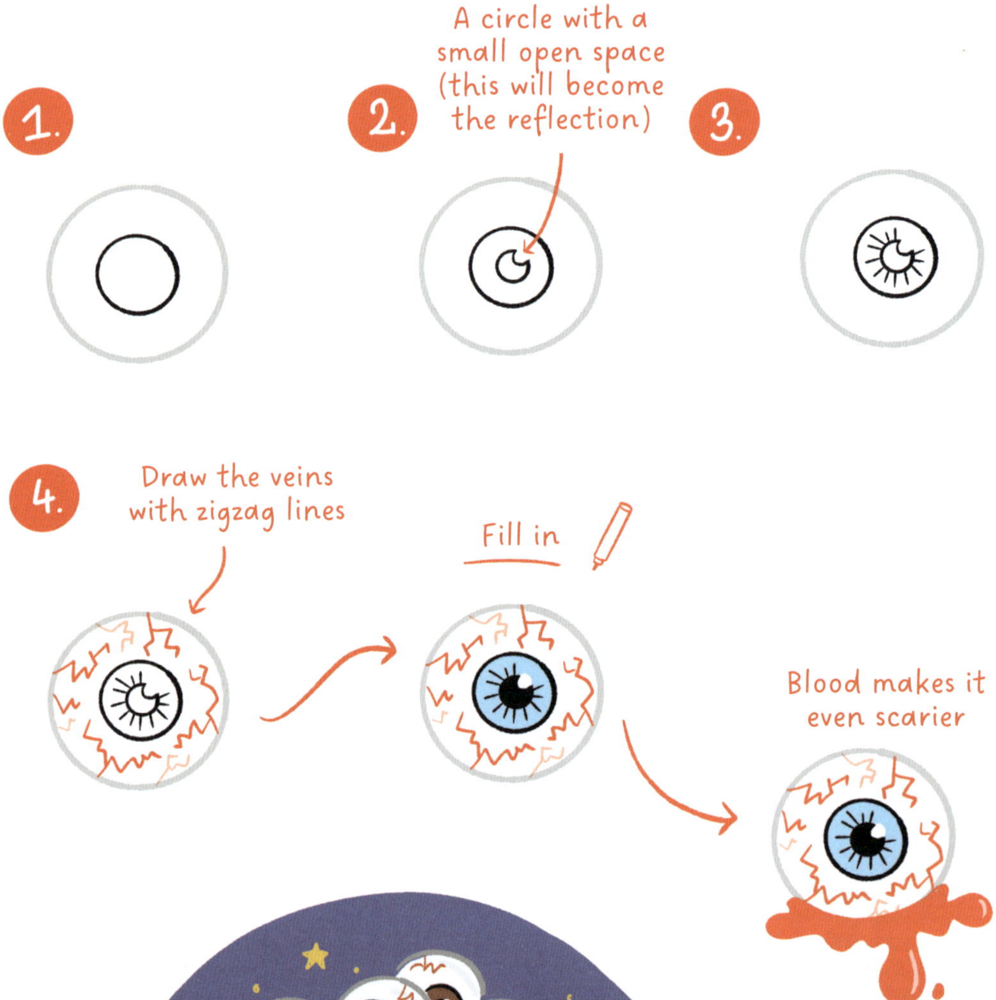

1.
2.
A circle with a small open space (this will become the reflection)
3.
4.
Draw the veins with zigzag lines
Fill in
Blood makes it even scarier

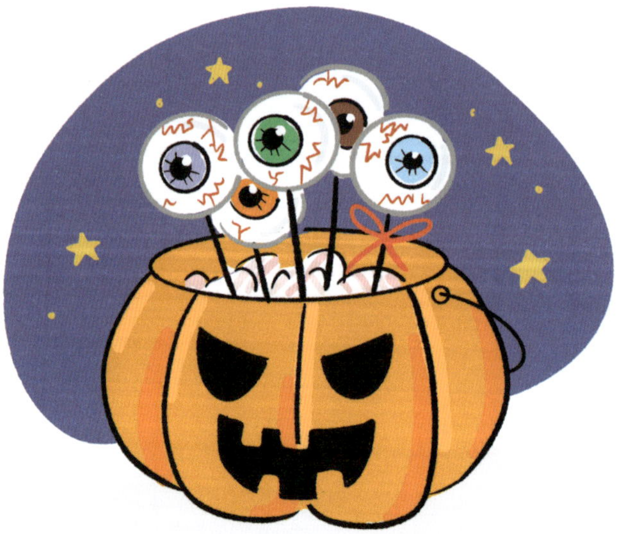

Cauldron

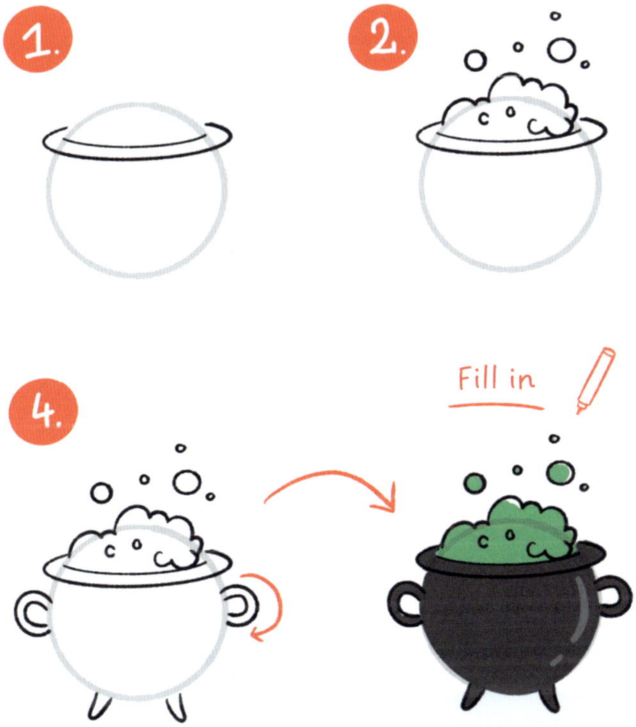

Flask

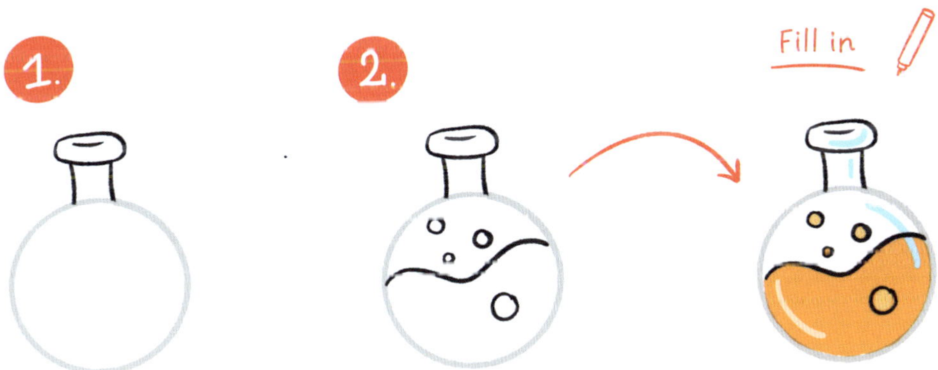

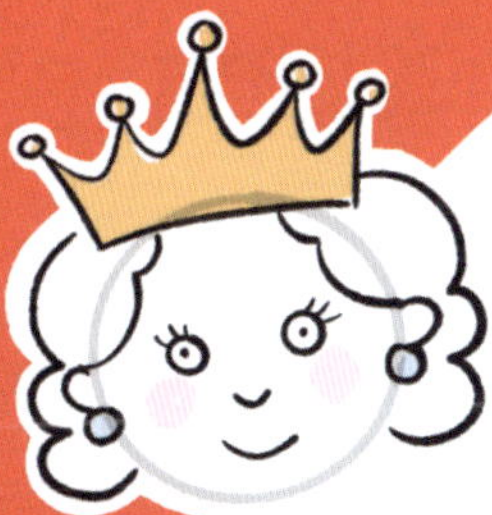

CHAPTER 3

People

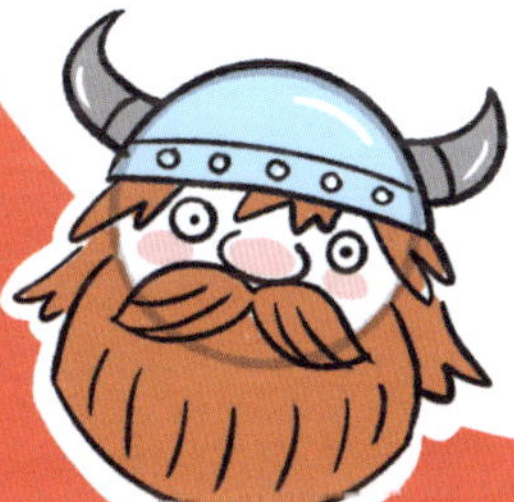
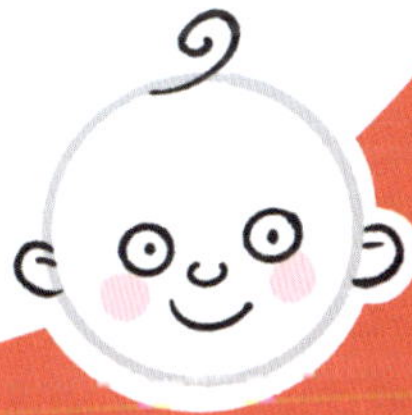

Faces and Emotions

To draw simple emotions, you don't need much more than circles, dots and lines for the mouth

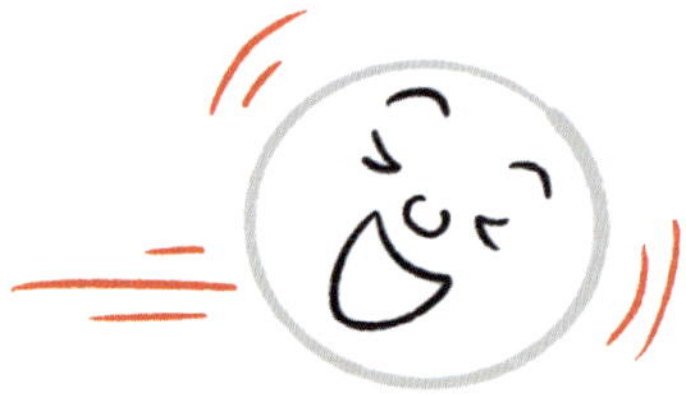

Satisfied

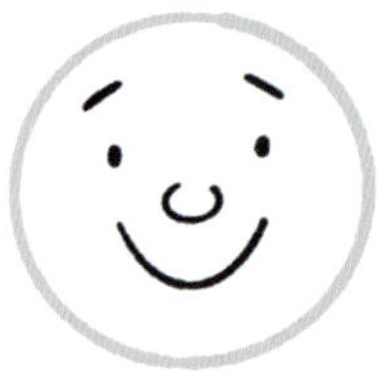

Happy

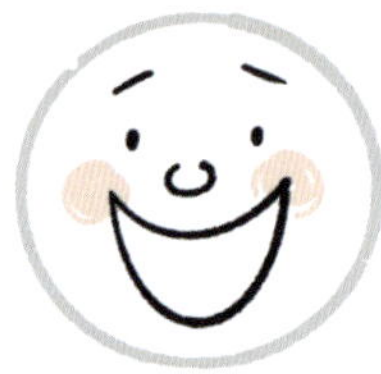

Excited

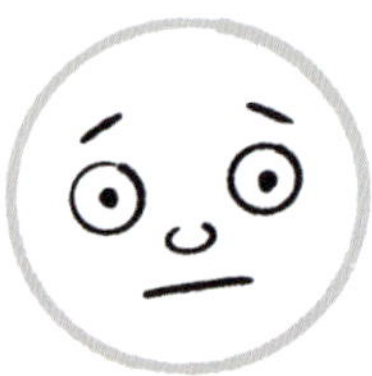

Worried

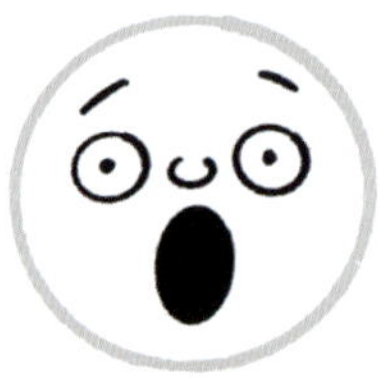

Shocked

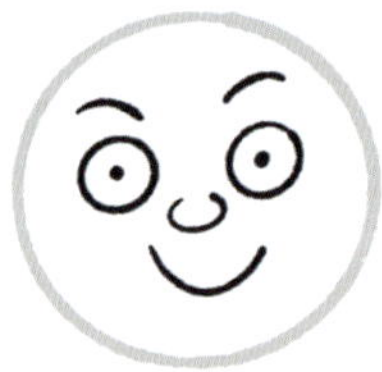

Evil

Grumpy

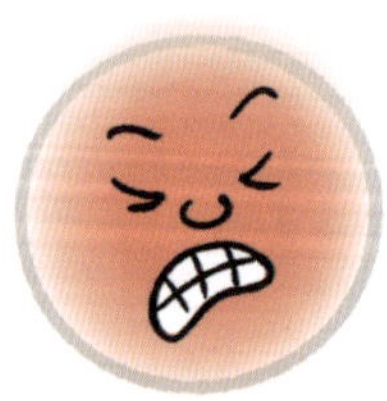

Angry

Crying

Hairstyles

To draw a whole head from a face, just add a hairstyle

Different hairstyles

Baby

1. Draw the ears slightly below the middle of the circle

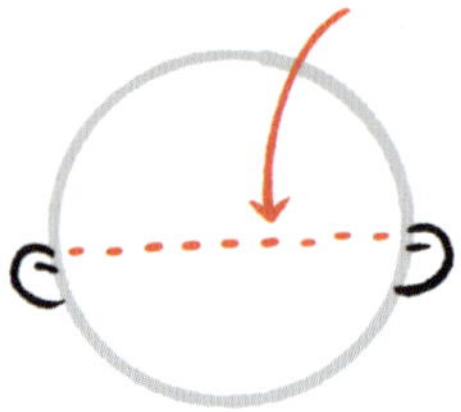

2. Draw the eyes at the level of the ears

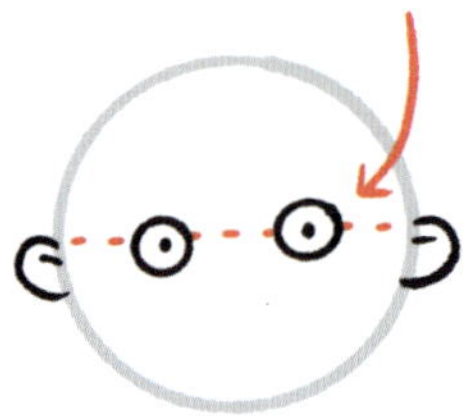

3. Draw a cute little nose

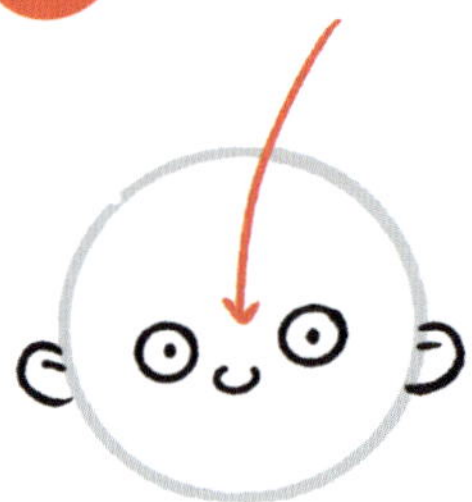

4.

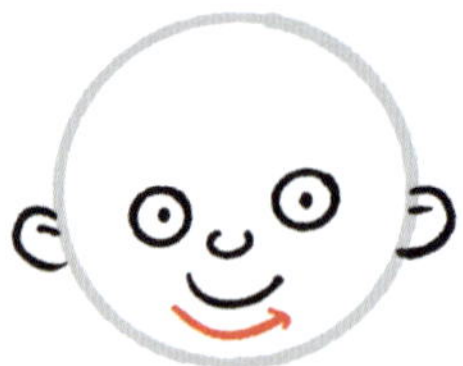

5. Draw a spiral as a curl

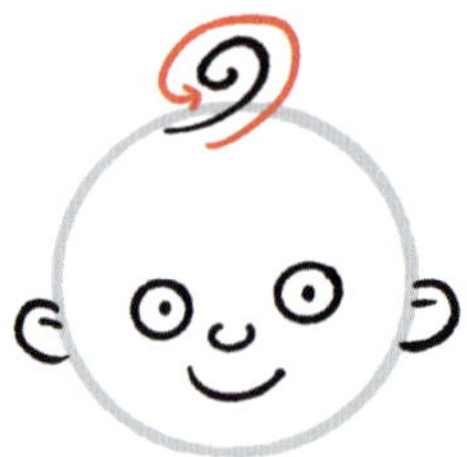

6. Pink cheeks make the face cuter

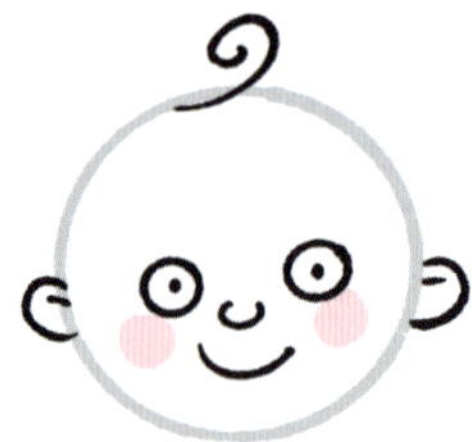

A few variations

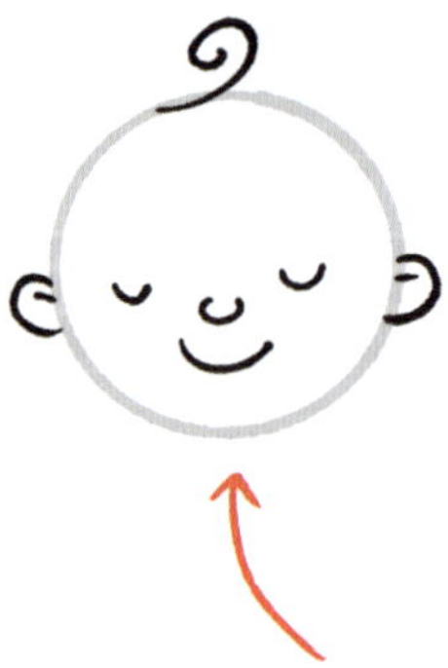

Content baby with closed eyes

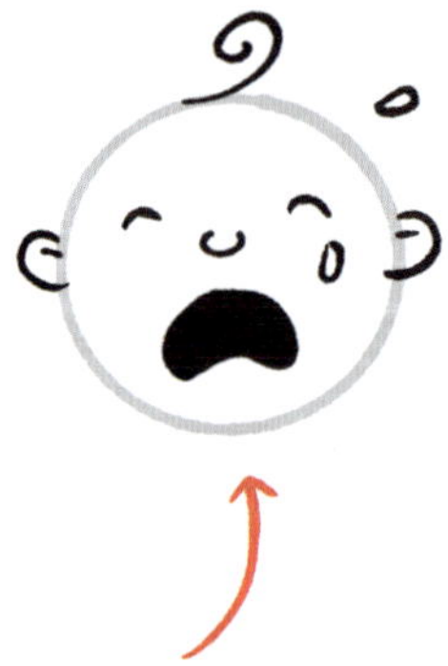

Crying baby with open mouth

With pacifier and swaddled

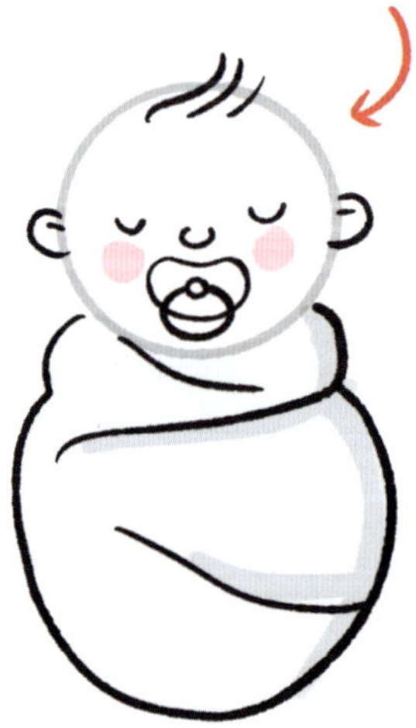

Astronaut

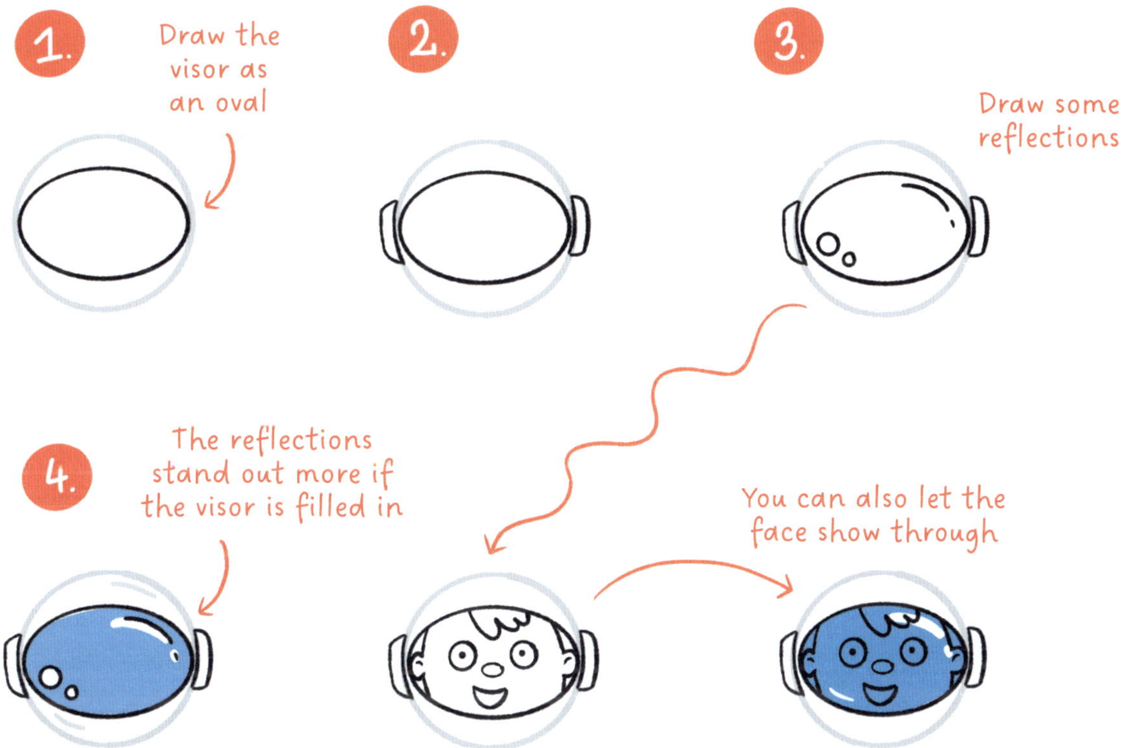
1.
Draw the visor as an oval
2.
3.
Draw some reflections
4.
The reflections stand out more if the visor is filled in
You can also let the face show through

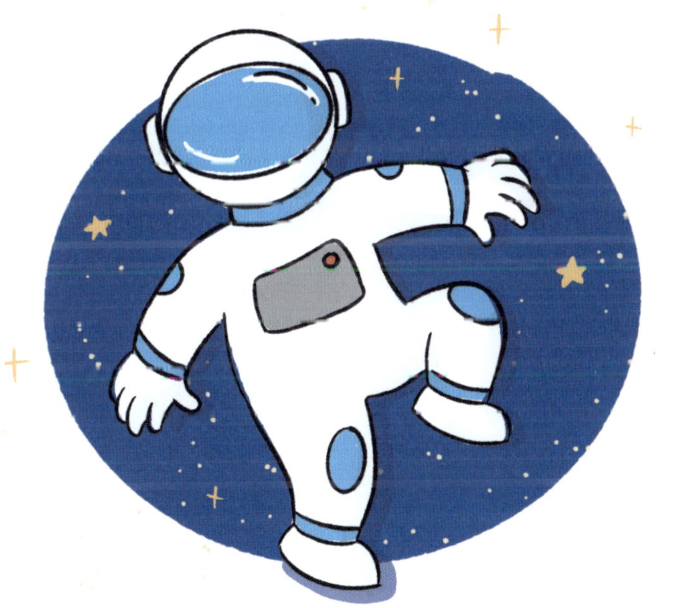

Clown

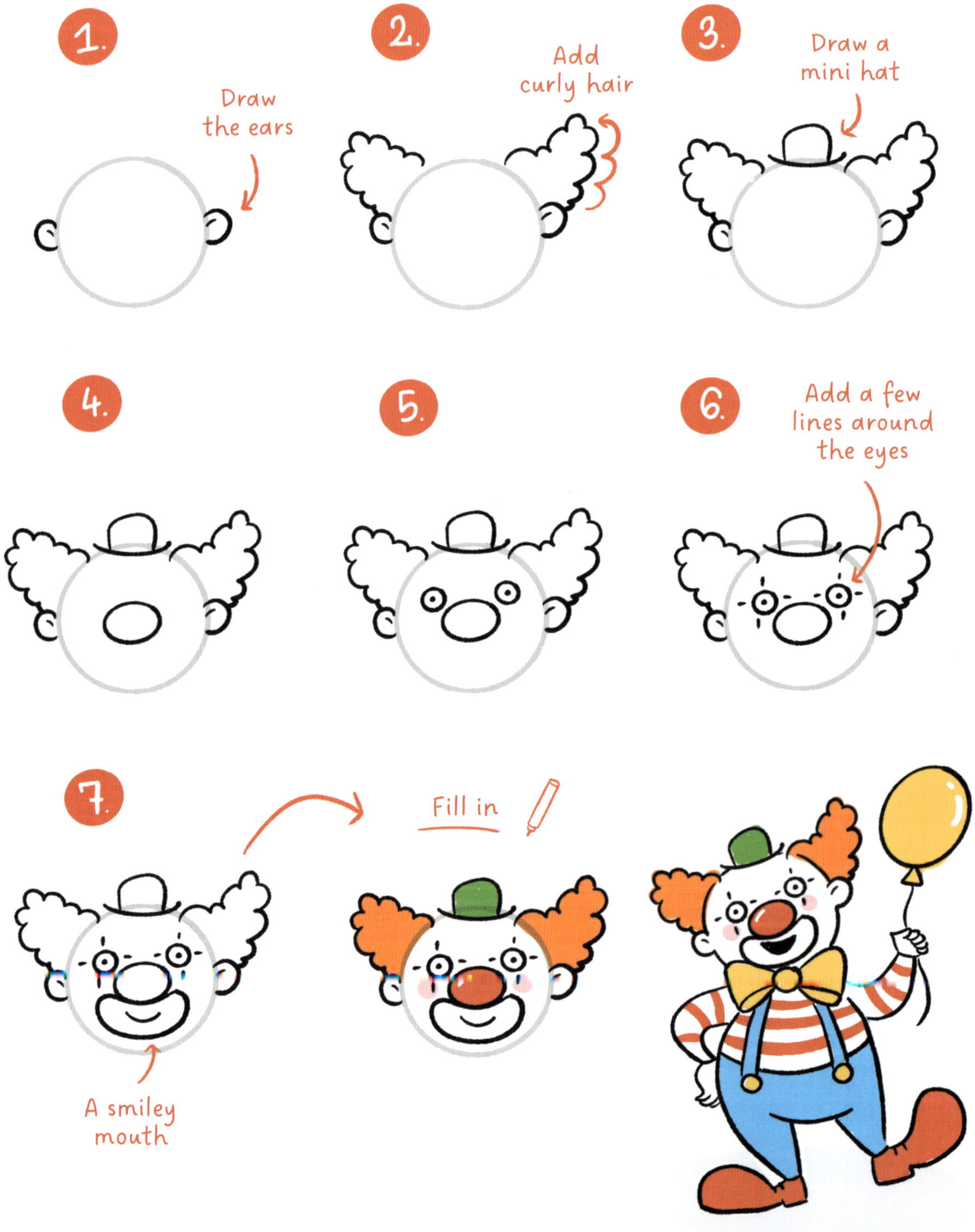
1.
Draw the ears
2.
Add curly hair
3.
Draw a mini hat
4.
5.
6.
Add a few lines around the eyes
7.
A smiley mouth
Fill in

Pirate

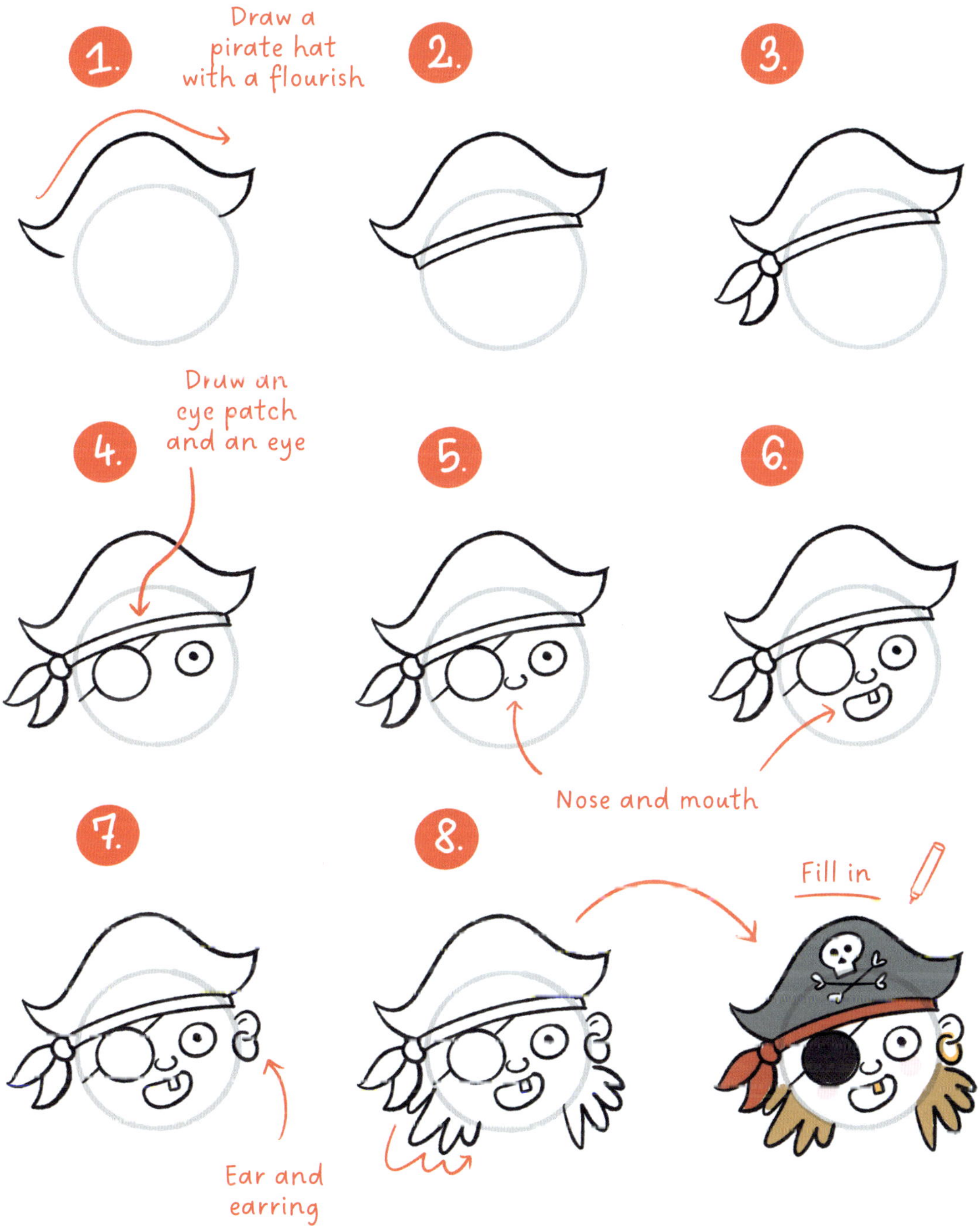
1.
Draw a pirate hat with a flourish
2.
3.
4.
Draw an eye patch and an eye
5.
6.
Nose and mouth
7.
Ear and earring
8.
Fill in

Angel

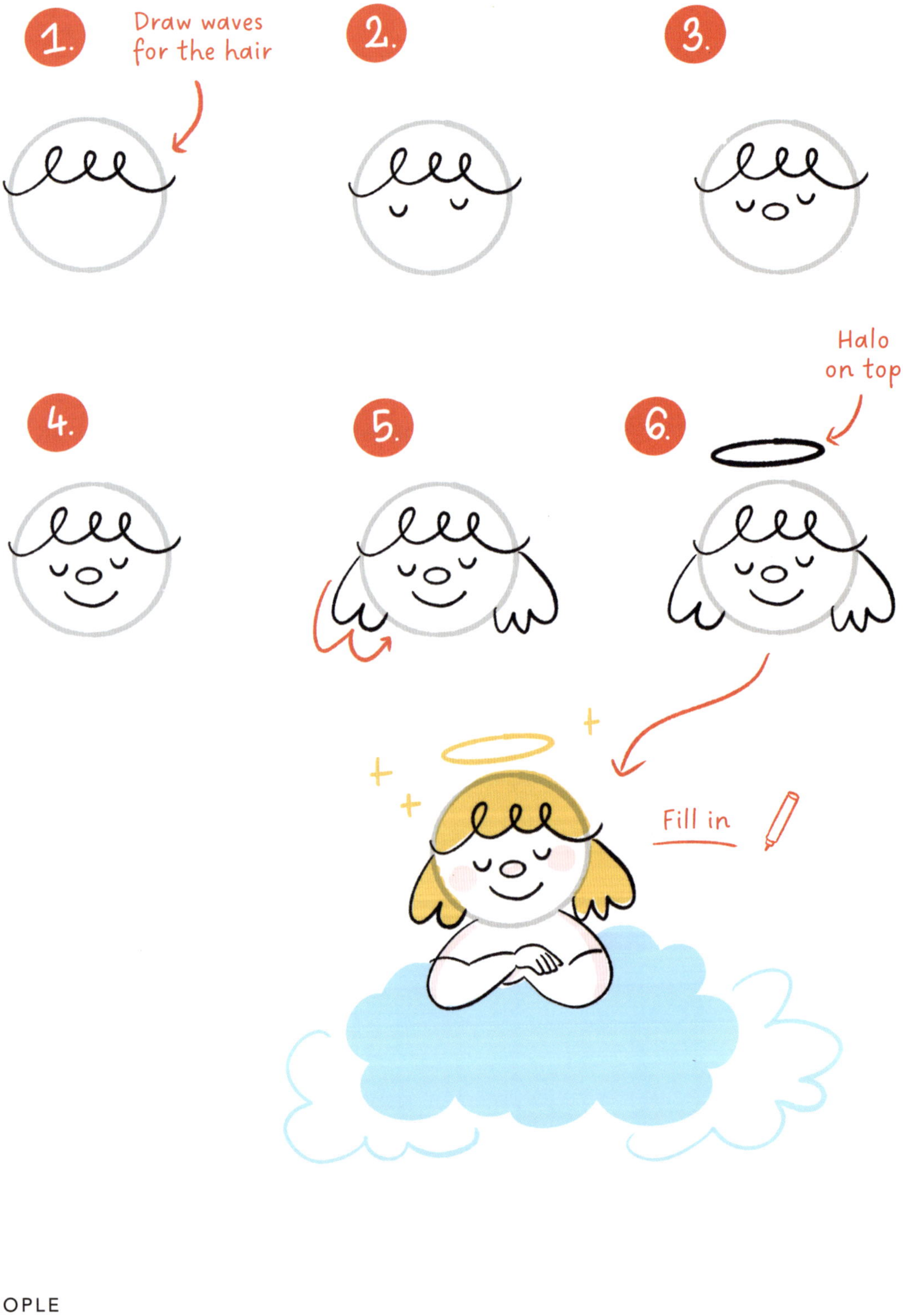

Devil

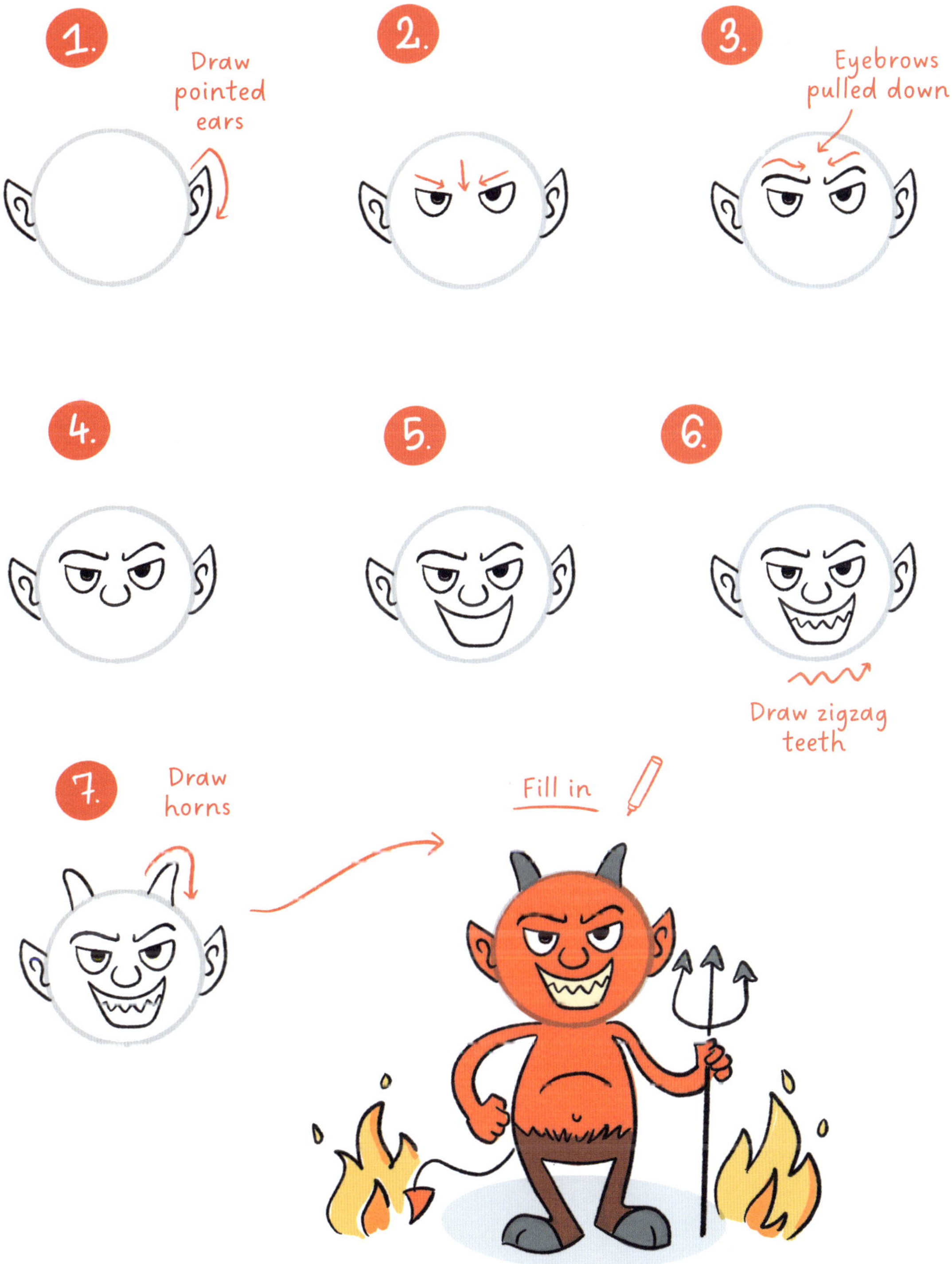
1.
Draw pointed ears
2.
3.
Eyebrows pulled down
4.
5.
6.
Draw zigzag teeth
7.
Draw horns
Fill in

Queen

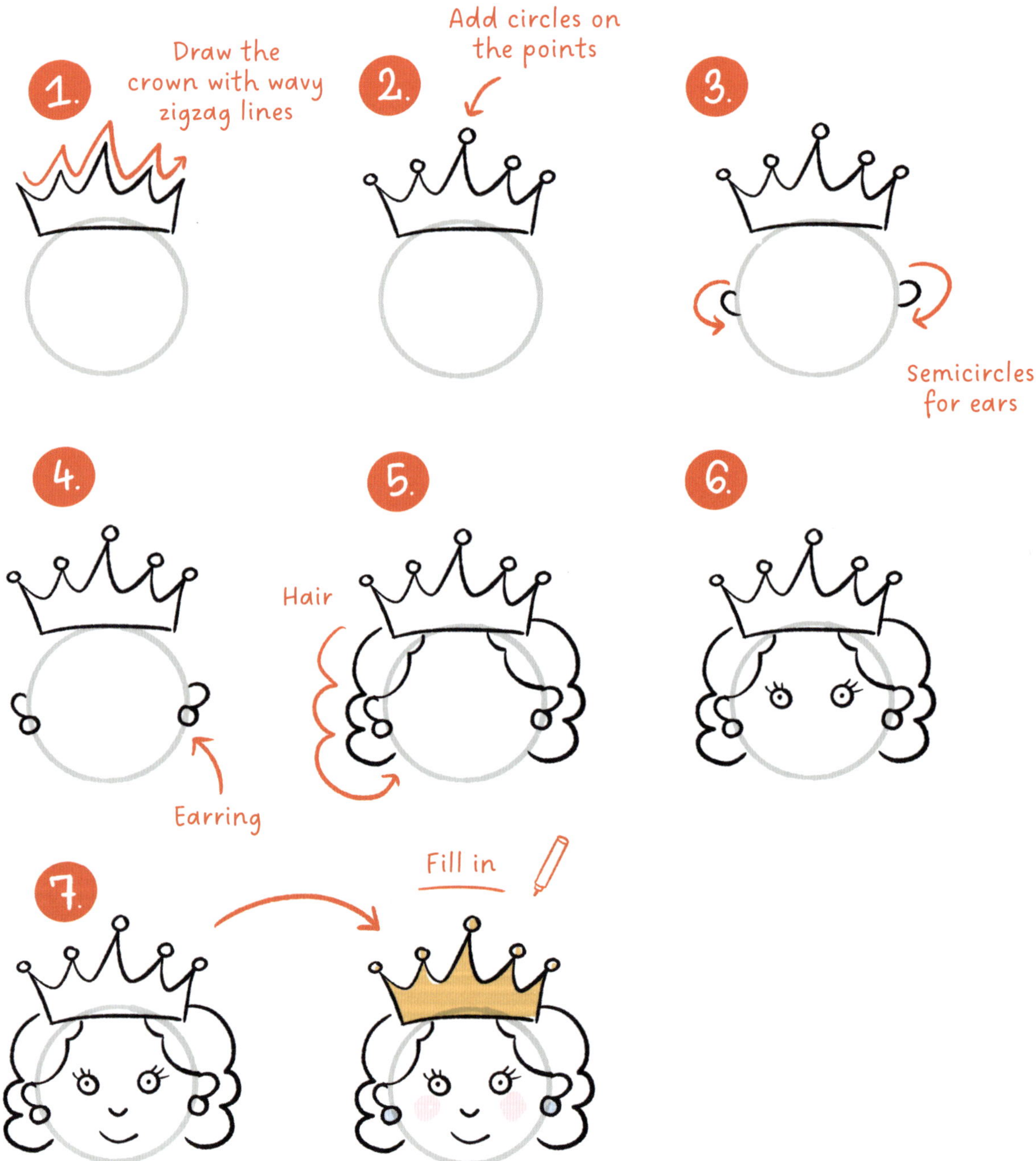

1.
Draw the crown with wavy zigzag lines
2.
Add circles on the points
3.
Semicircles for ears
4.
Earring
5.
Hair
6.
7.
Fill in

King

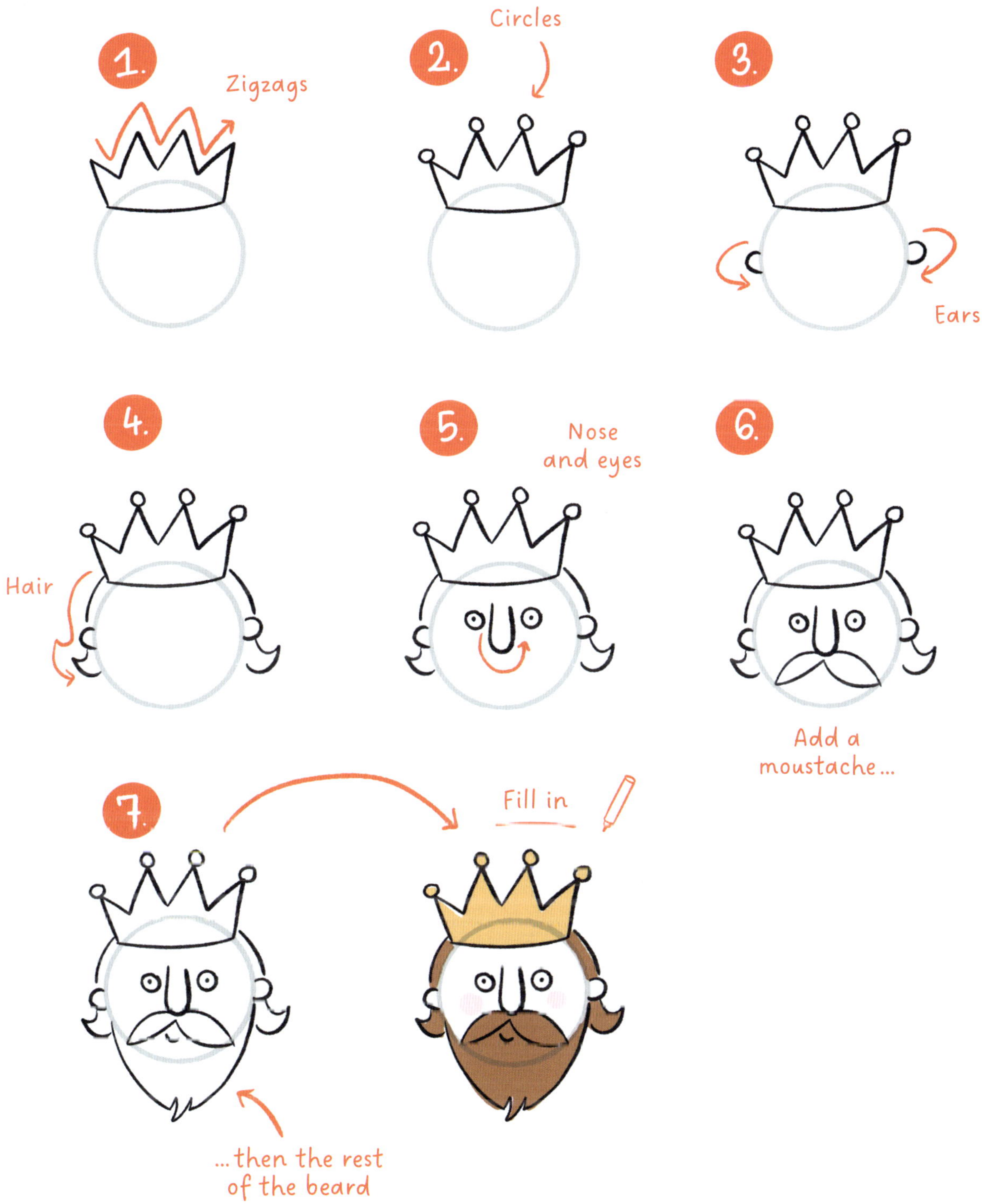
1.
Zigzags
2.
Circles
3.
Ears
4.
Hair
5.
Nose and eyes
6.
Add a moustache...
7.
...then the rest of the beard
Fill in

Grandfather

1.

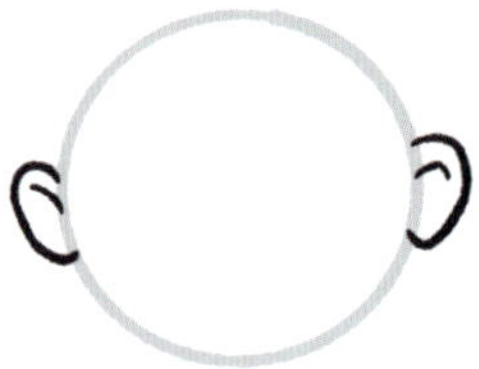

2.

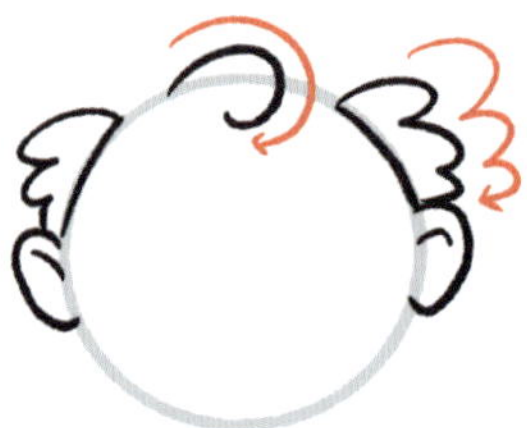

3.

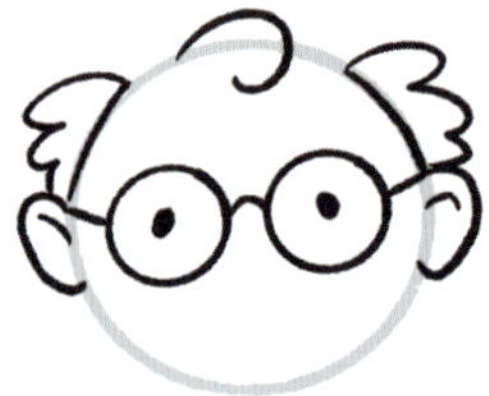

4.

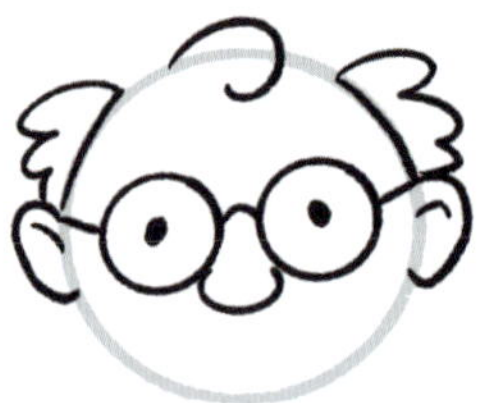

5.

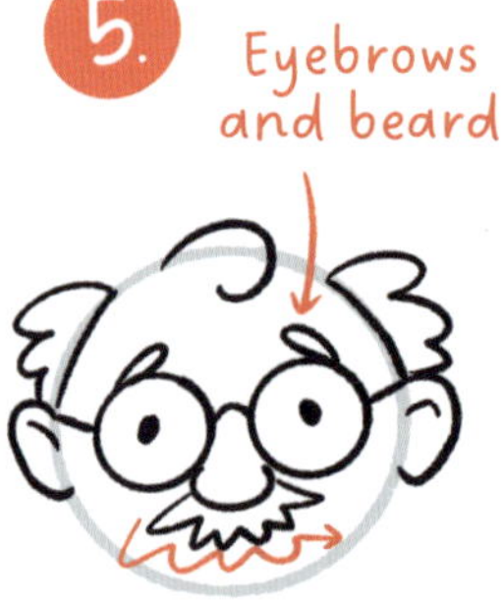

6.

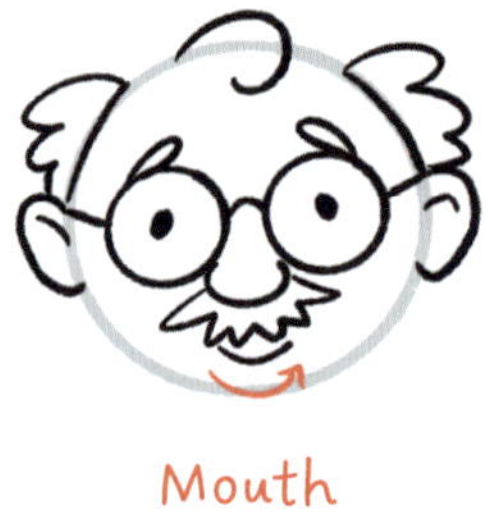

7.

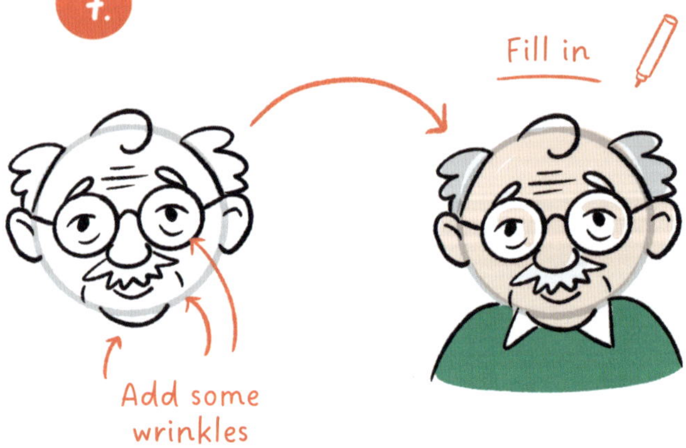

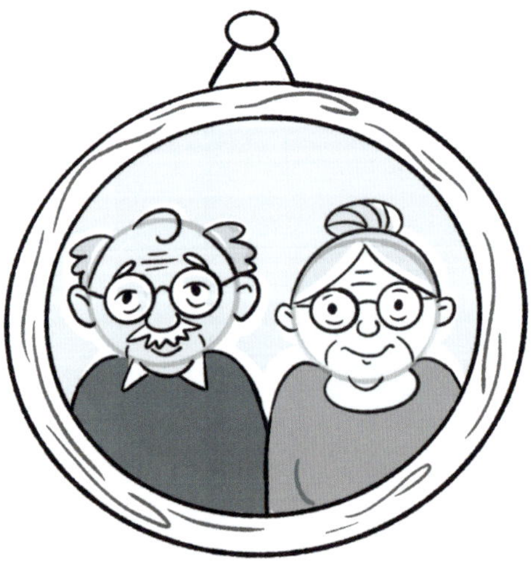

Grandmother

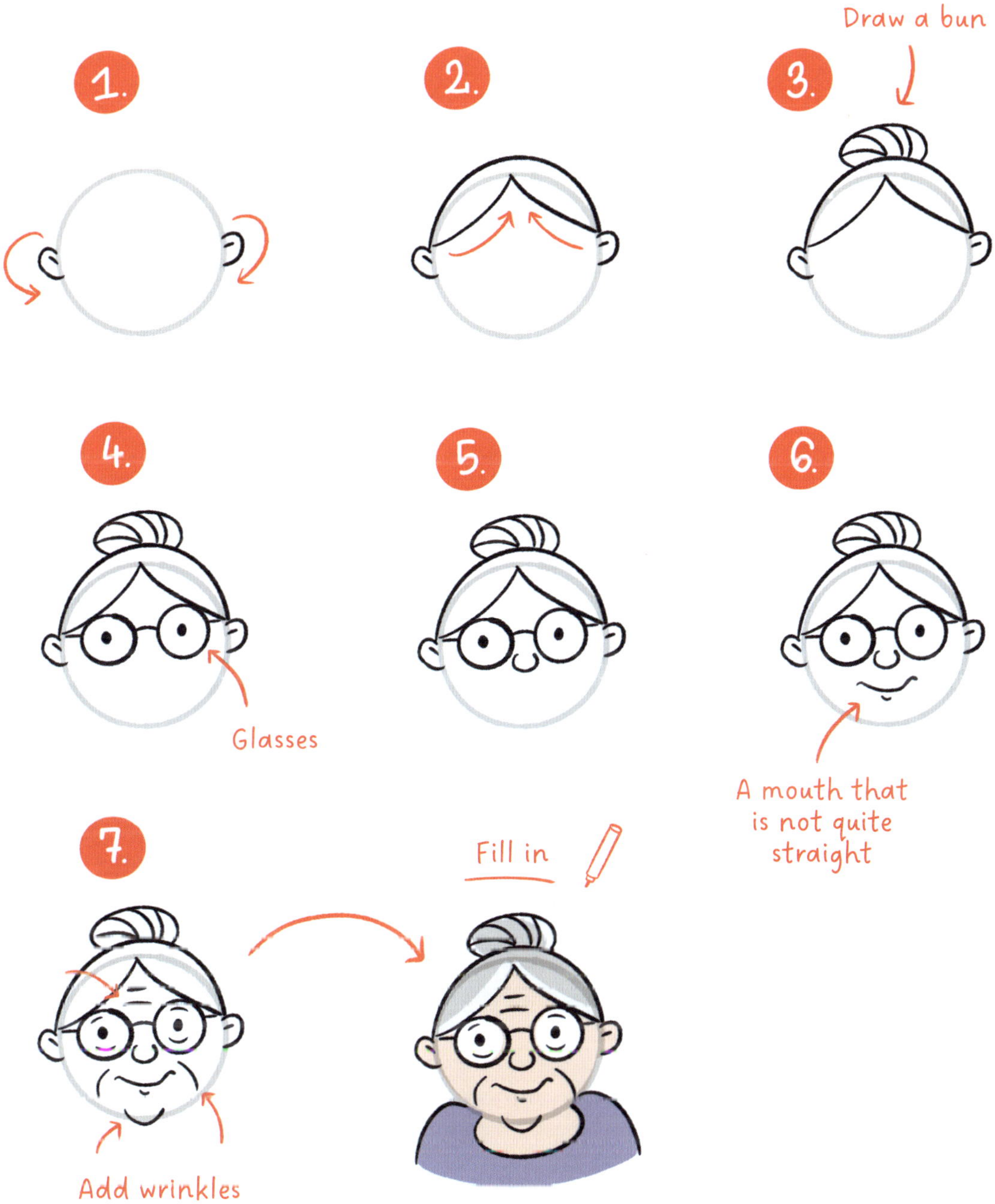

Monster

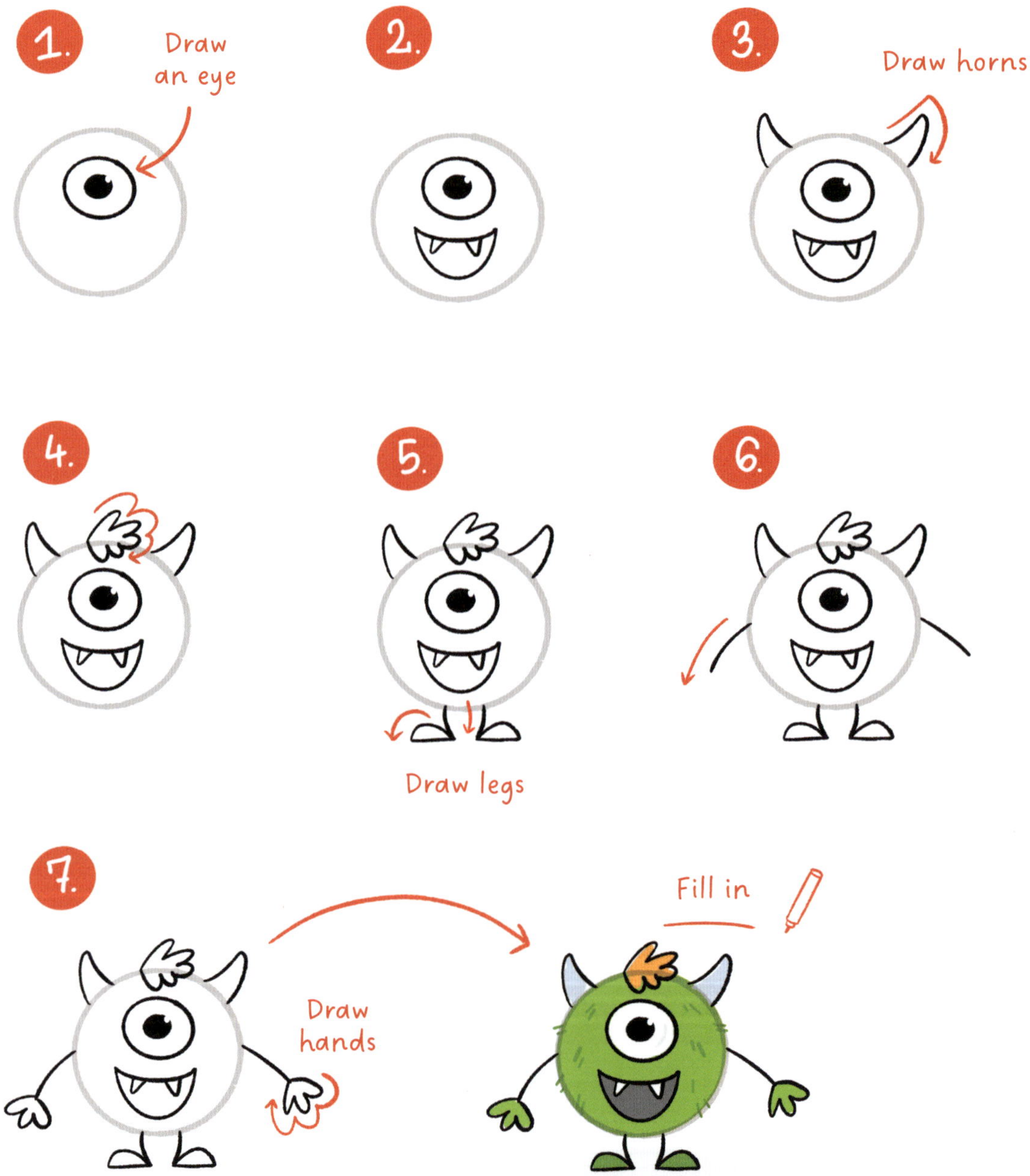

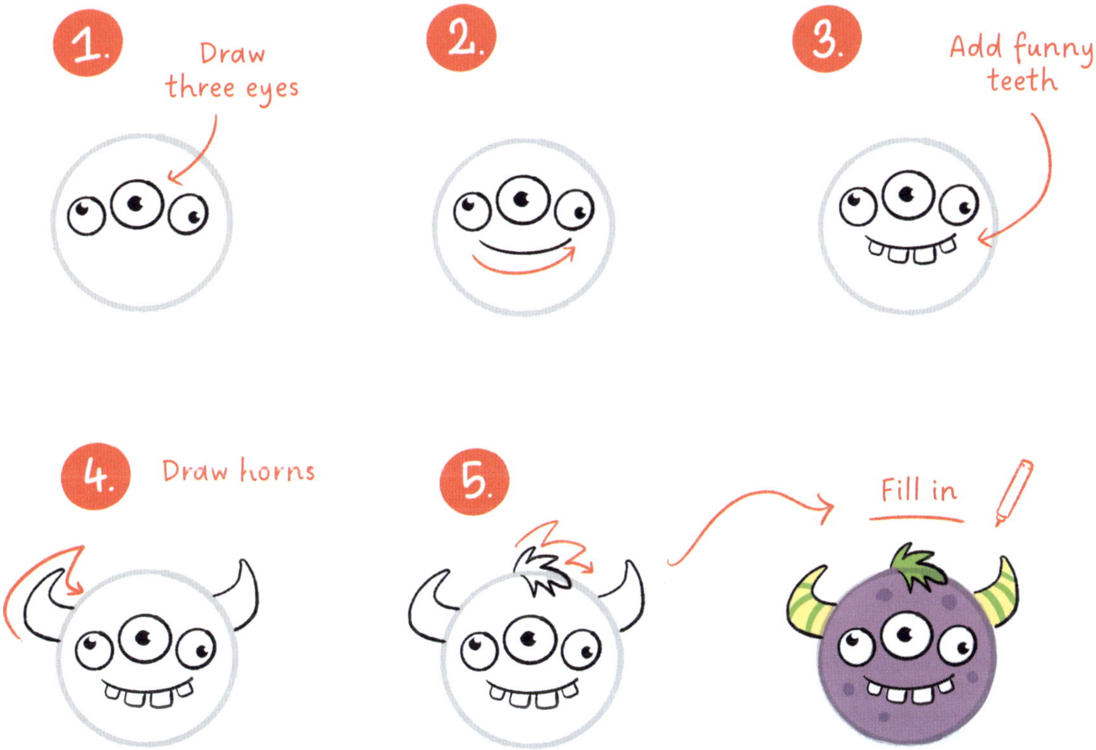

A few variations

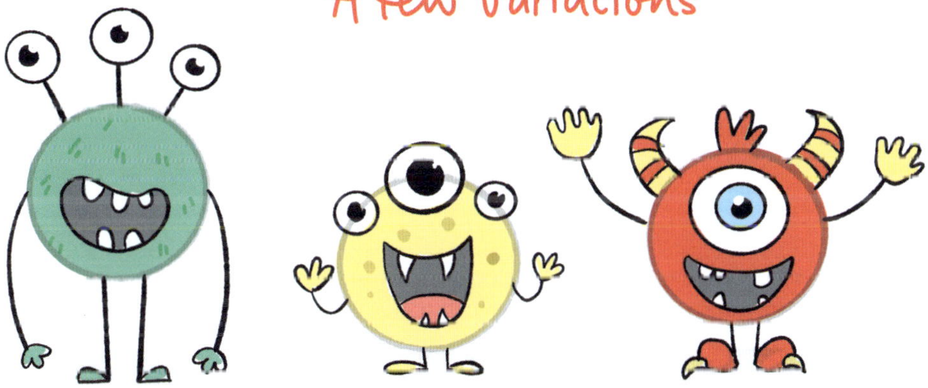

Witch

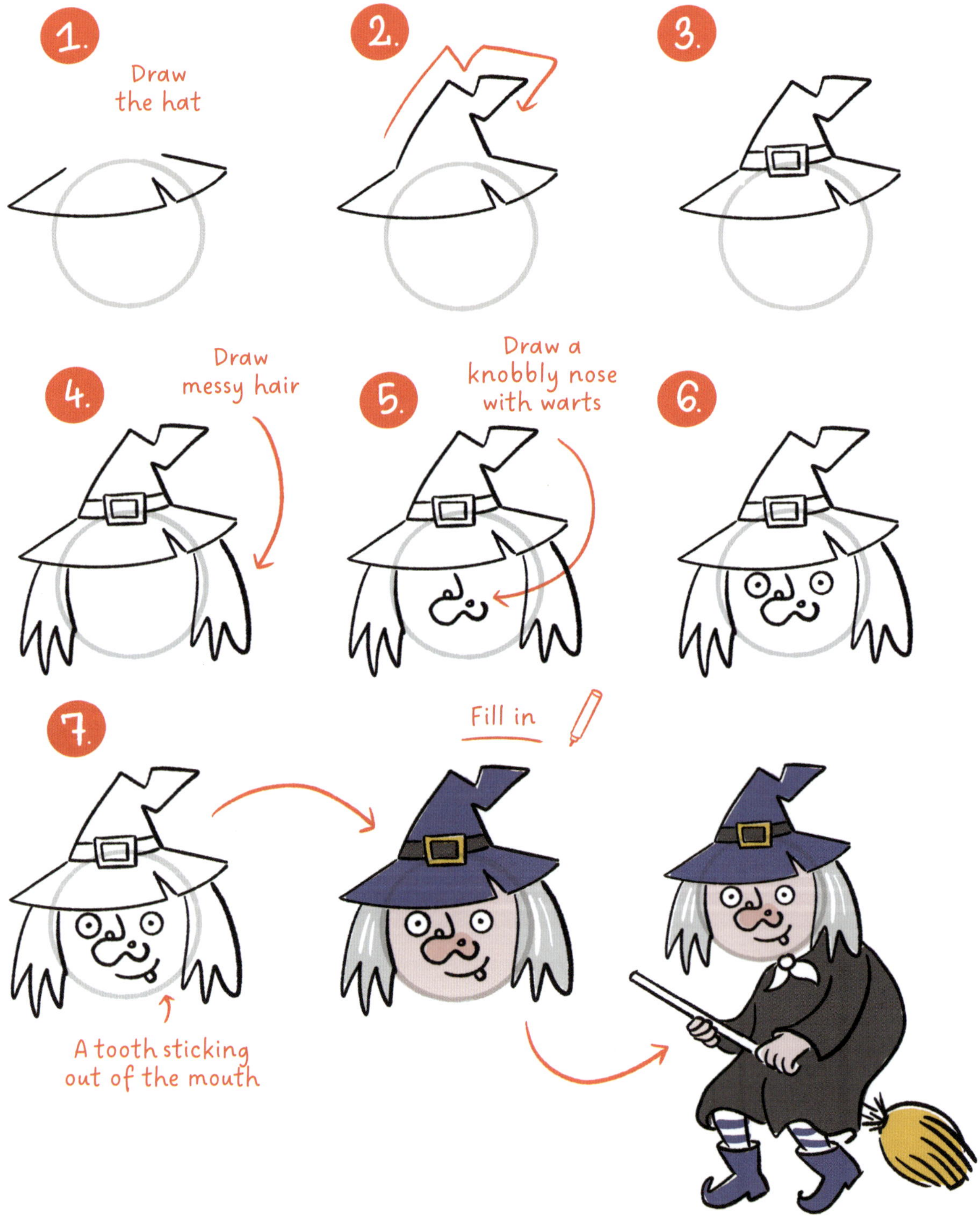
1.
Draw the hat
2.
3.
4.
Draw messy hair
5.
Draw a knobbly nose with warts
6.
7.
A tooth sticking out of the mouth
Fill in

Vampire

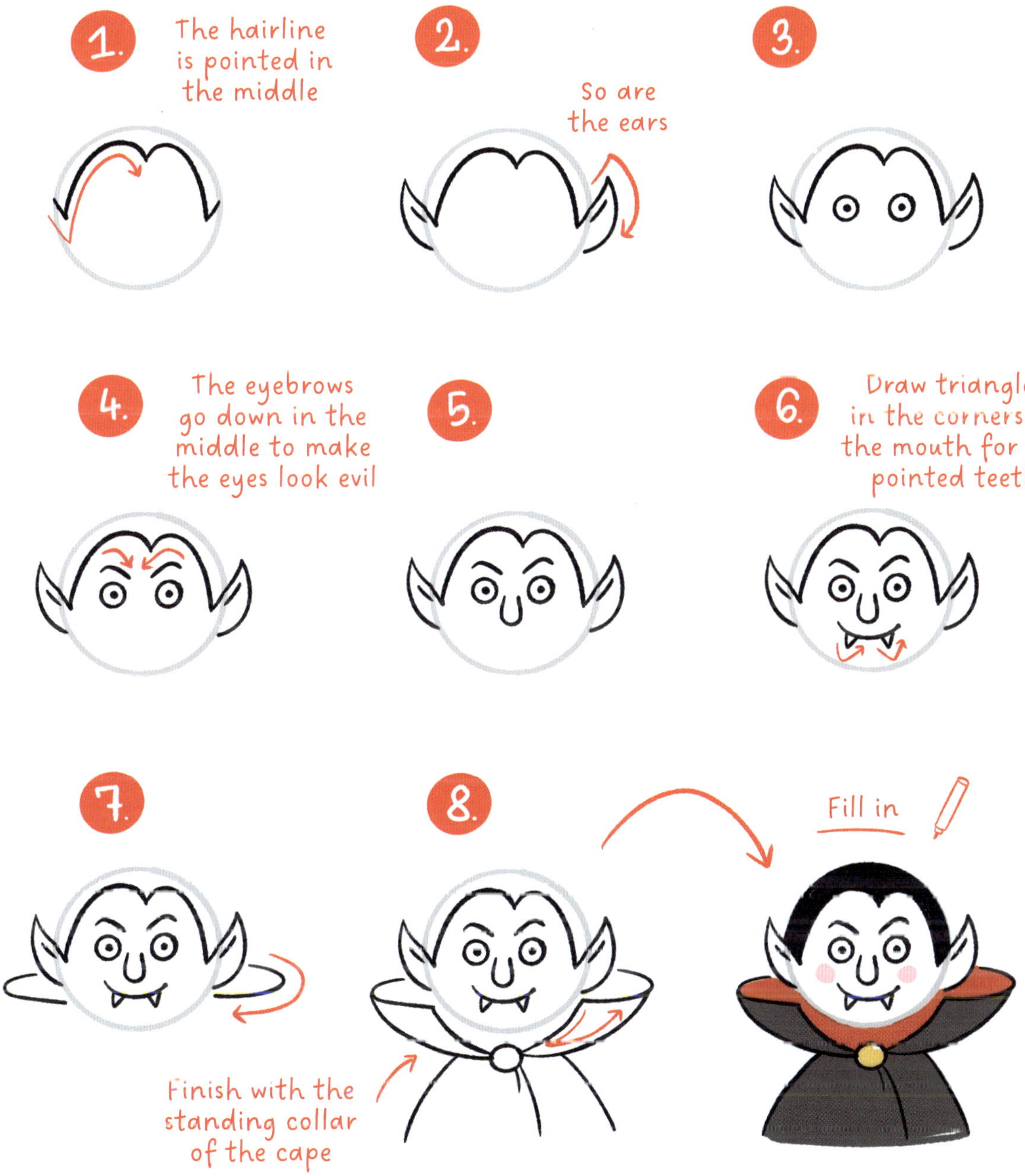
1.
The hairline is pointed in the middle
2.
So are the ears
3.
4.
The eyebrows go down in the middle to make the eyes look evil
5.
6.
Draw triangles in the corners of the mouth for the pointed teeth
7.
8.
Finish with the standing collar of the cape
Fill in

Superhero

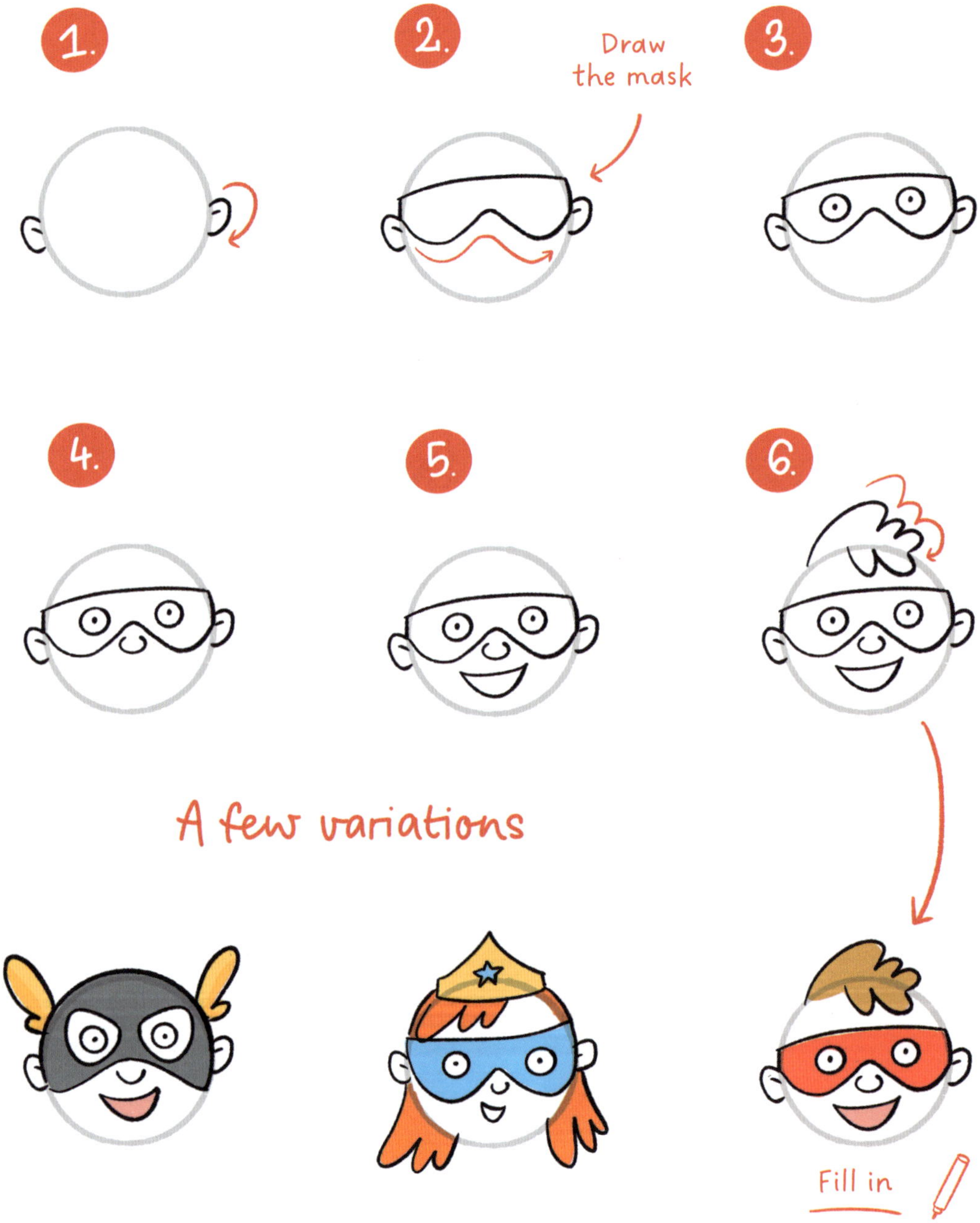

Ninja

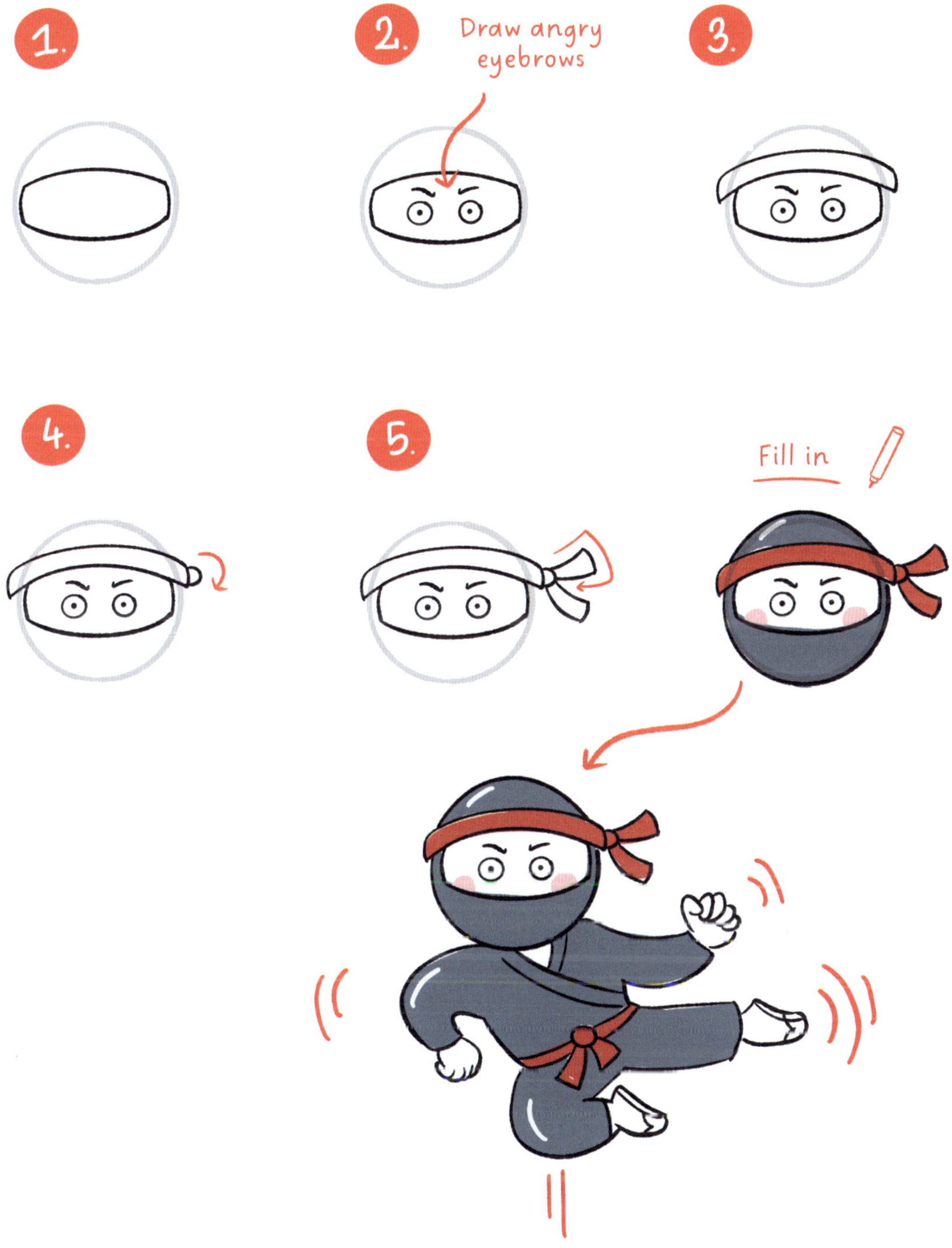

Skull

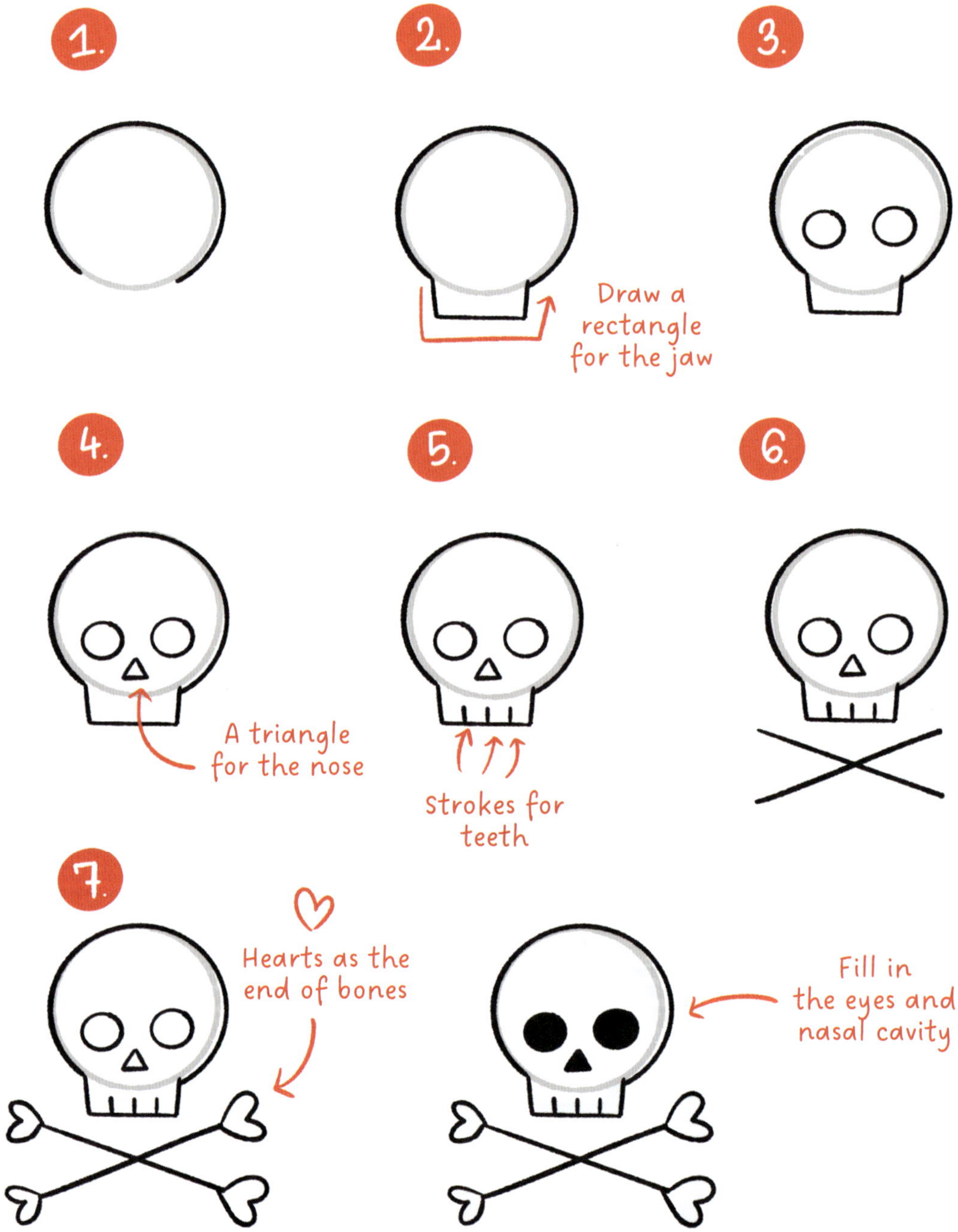
1.
2.
3.
Draw a rectangle for the jaw
4.
5.
6.
A triangle for the nose
Strokes for teeth
7.
Hearts as the end of bones
Fill in the eyes and nasal cavity

Viking

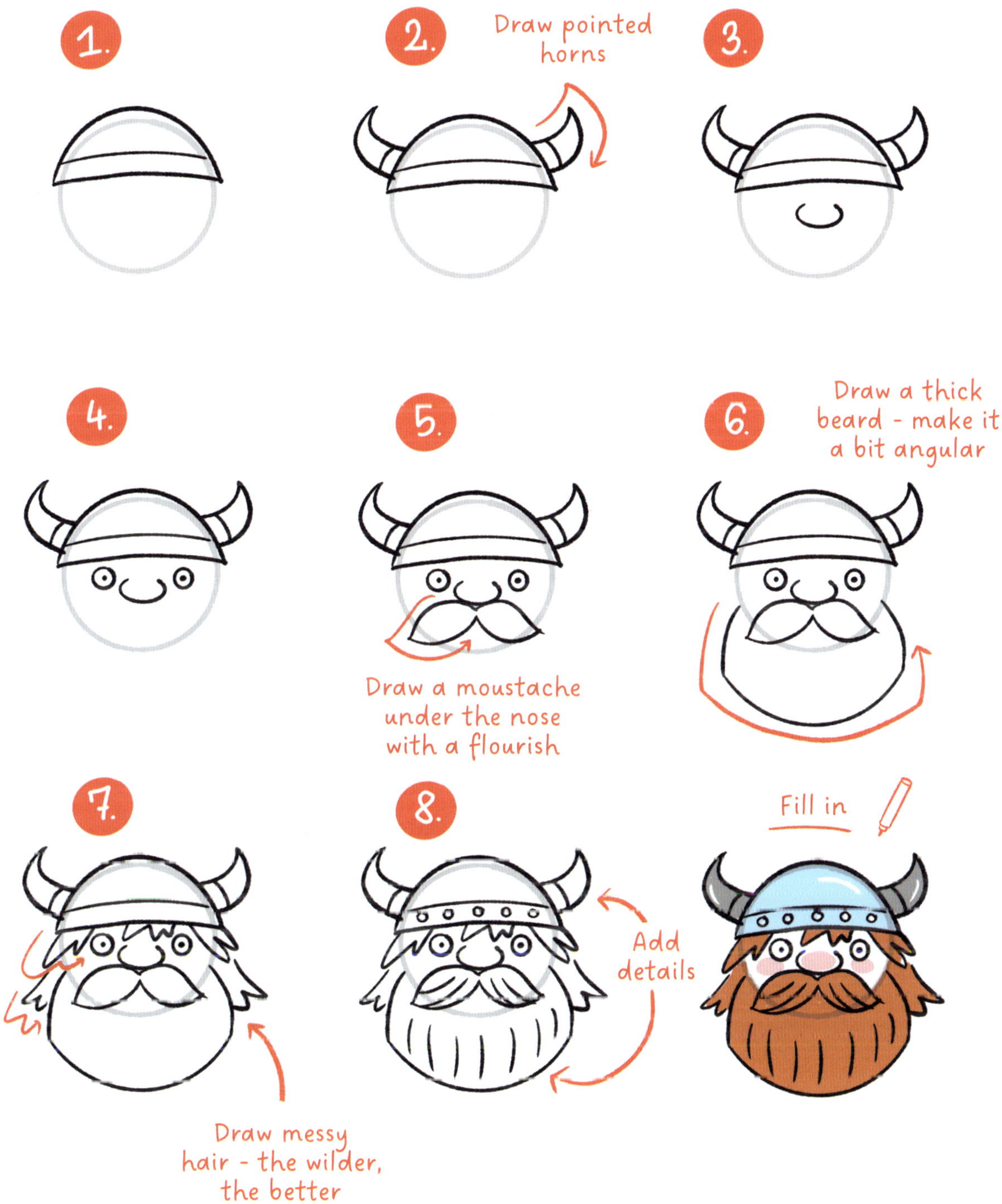
1.
2.
Draw pointed horns
3.
4.
5.
Draw a moustache under the nose with a flourish
6.
Draw a thick beard - make it a bit angular
7.
Draw messy hair - the wilder, the better
8.
Add details
Fill in

CHAPTER 4

Food

Donut

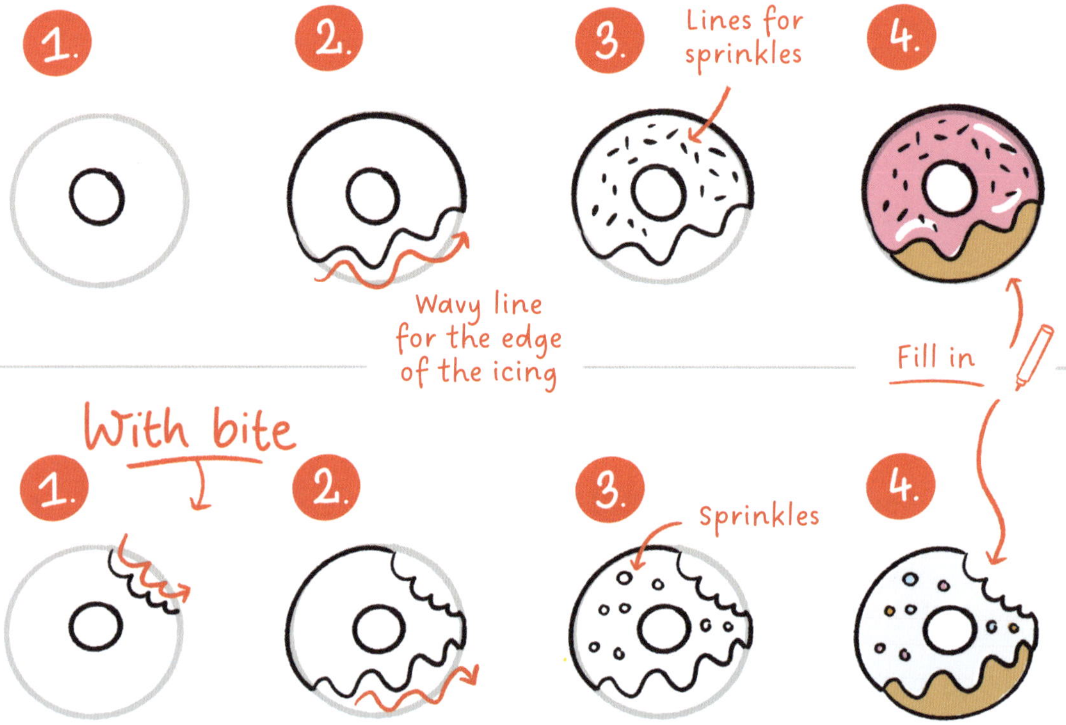

A few variations

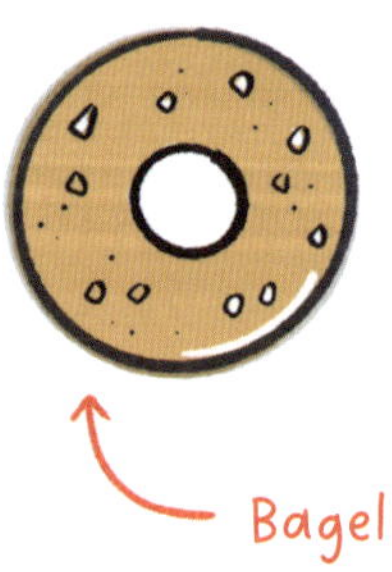

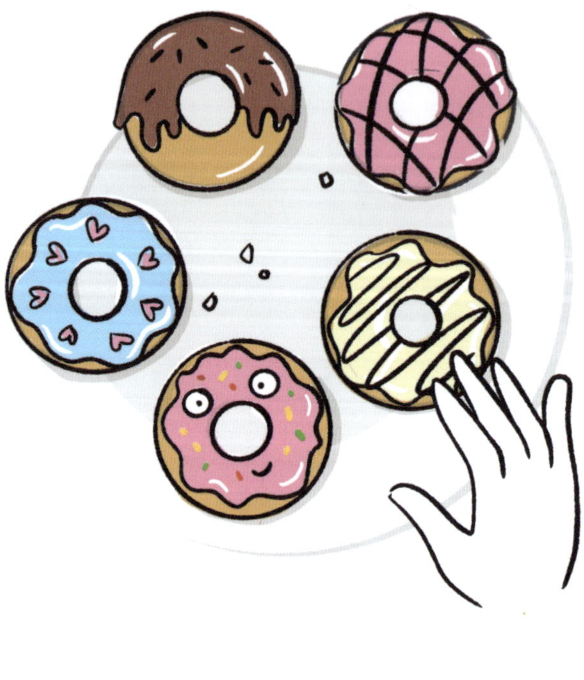

Cinnamon roll

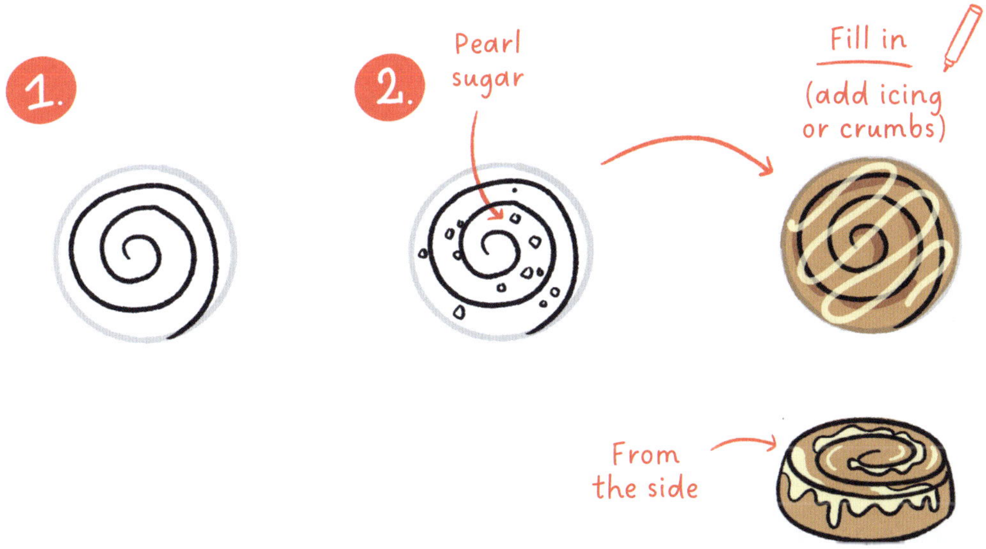

Cookies

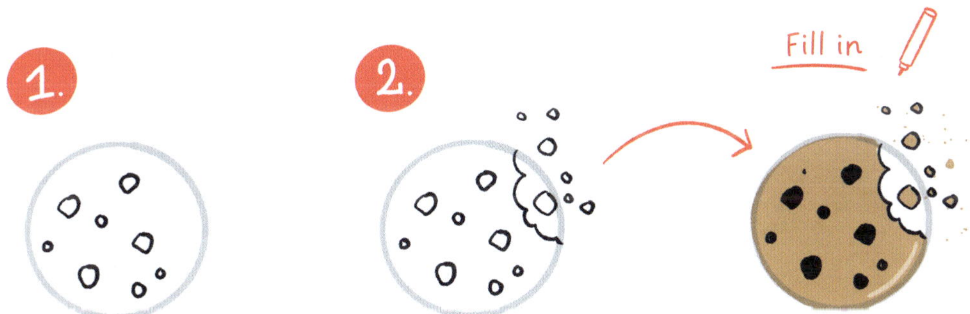

Variations

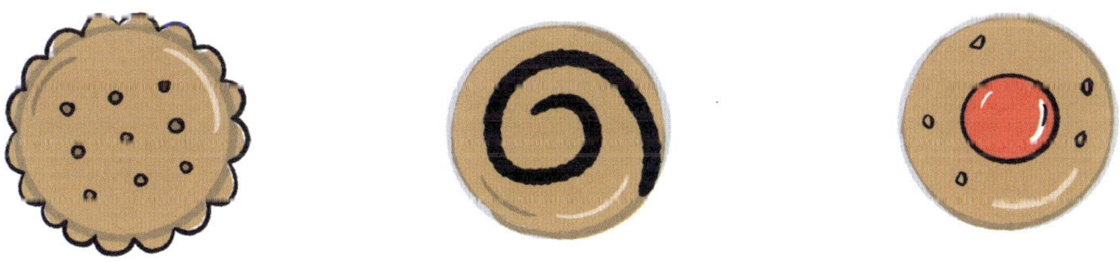

Ice cream

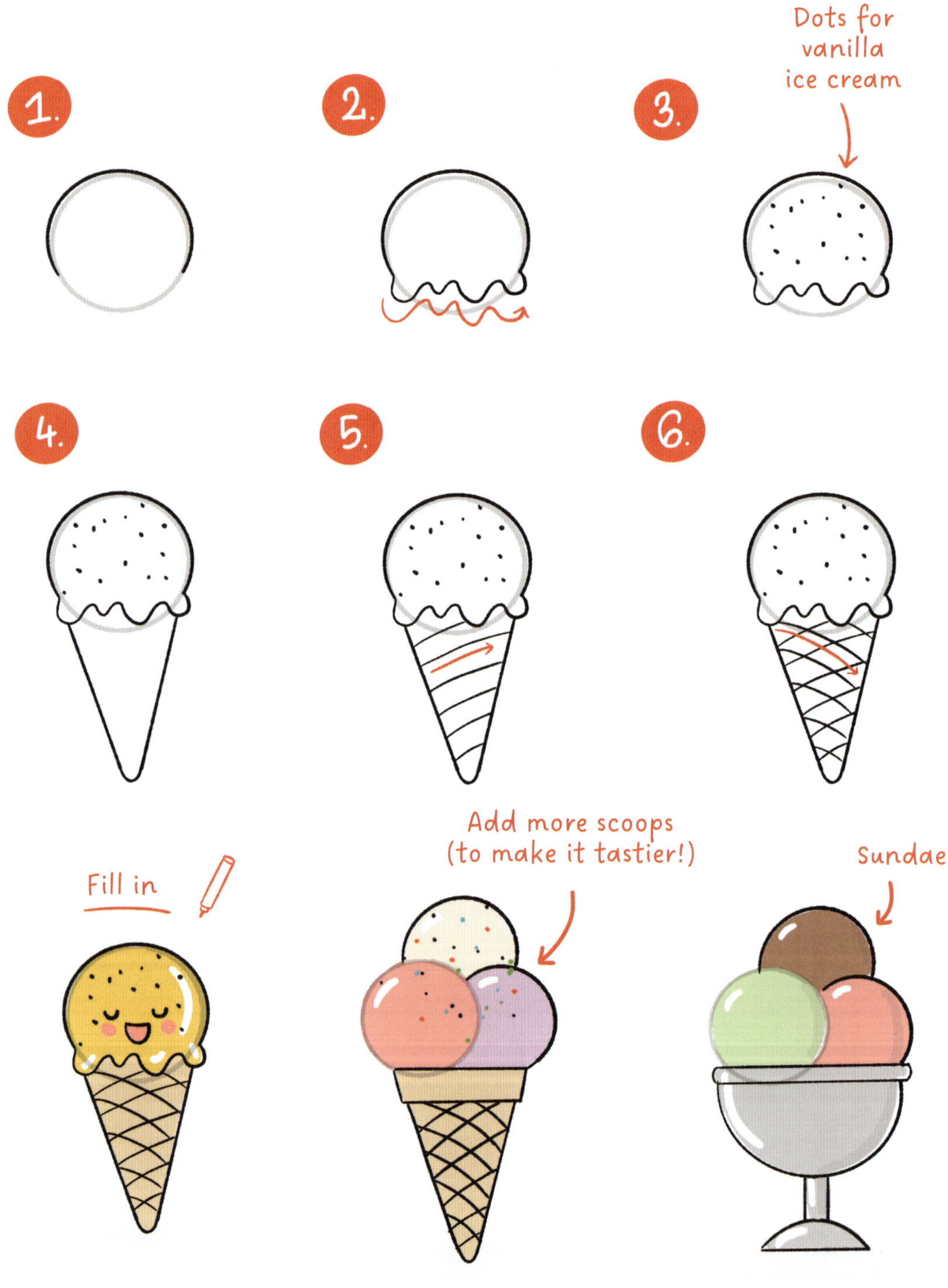

Dots for vanilla ice cream
1.
2.
3.
4.
5.
6.
Fill in
Add more scoops (to make it tastier!)
Sundae

Lollipop

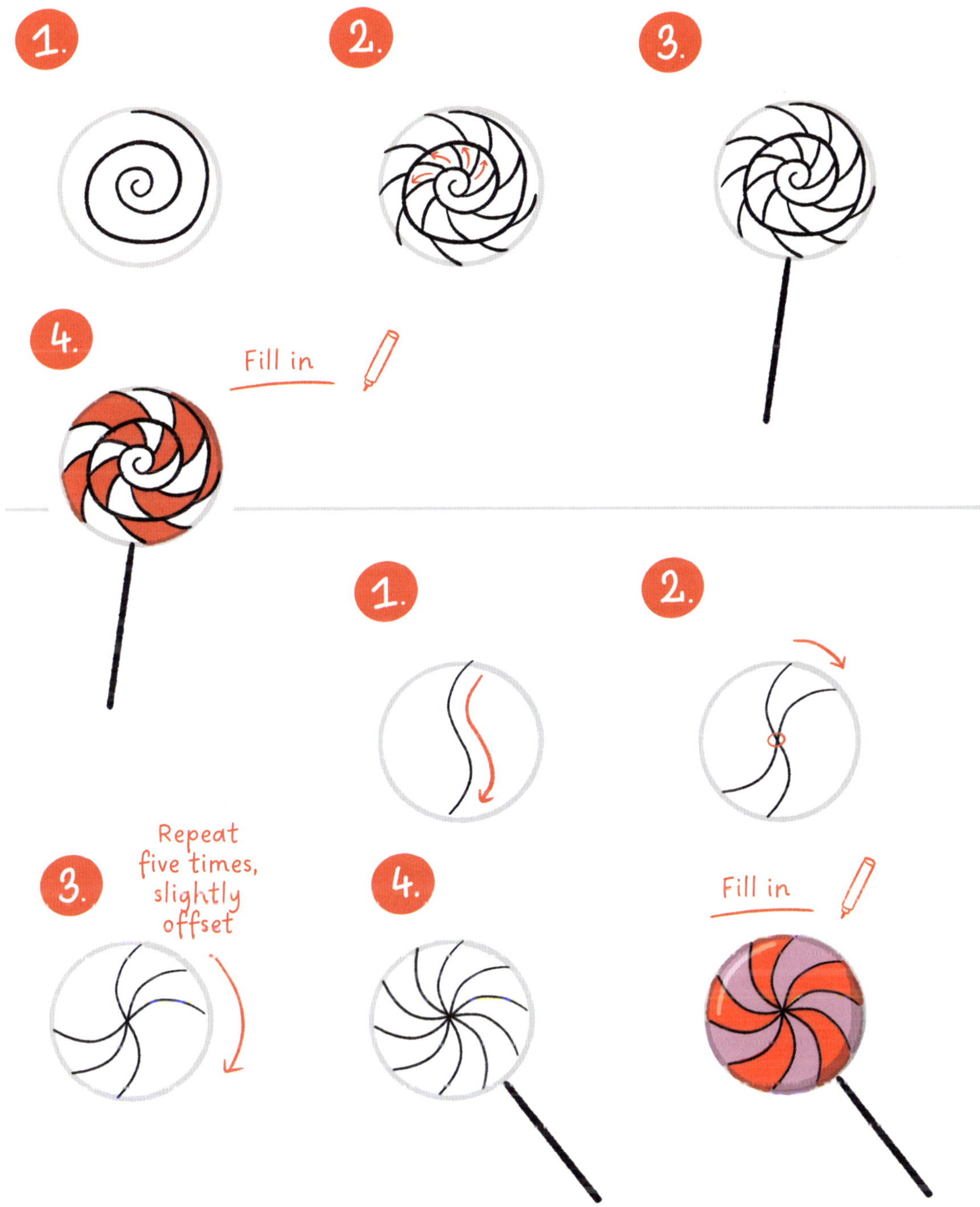

Pizza

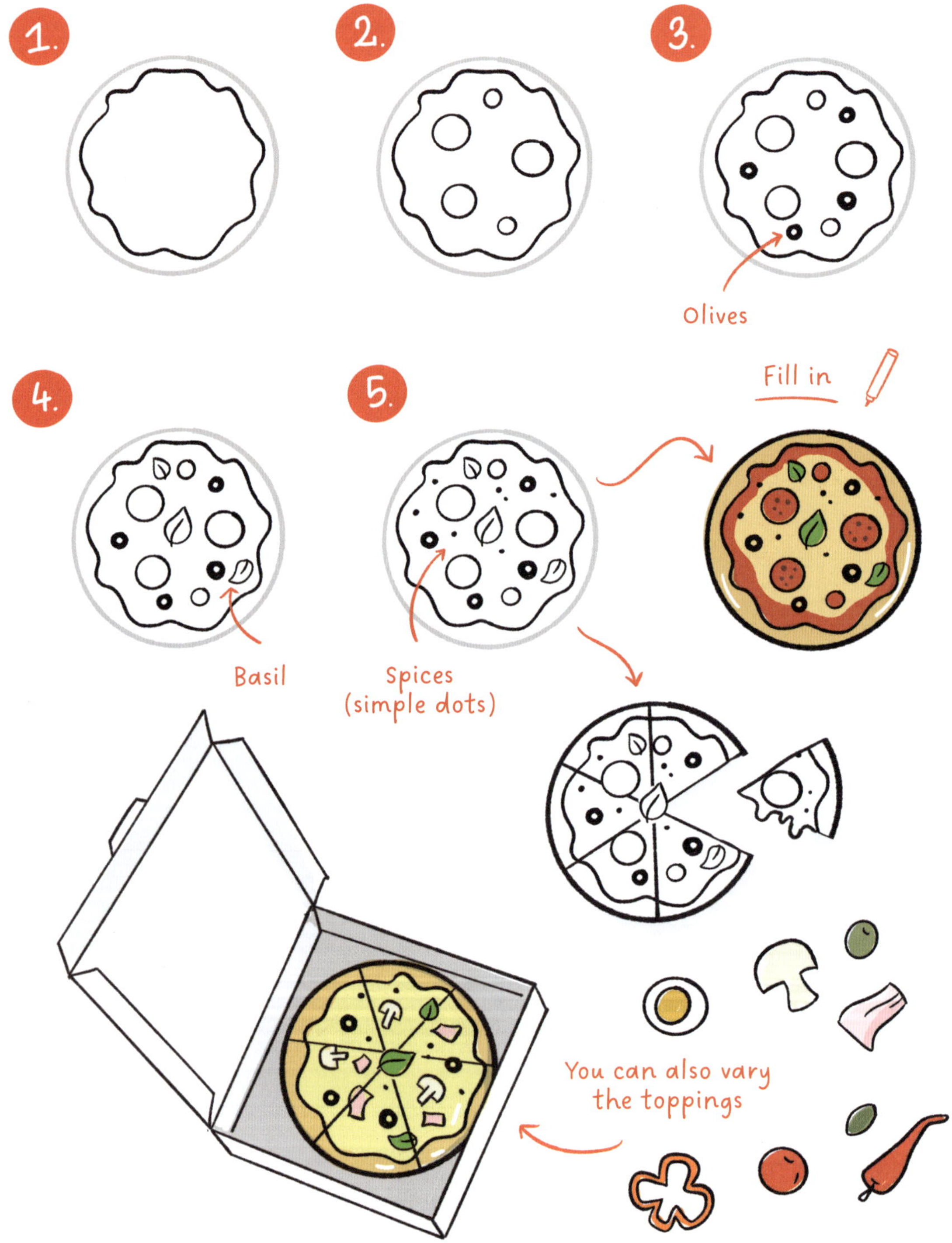
1.
2.
3.
Olives
4.
5.
Fill in
Basil
Spices
(simple dots)
You can also vary
the toppings

Avocado

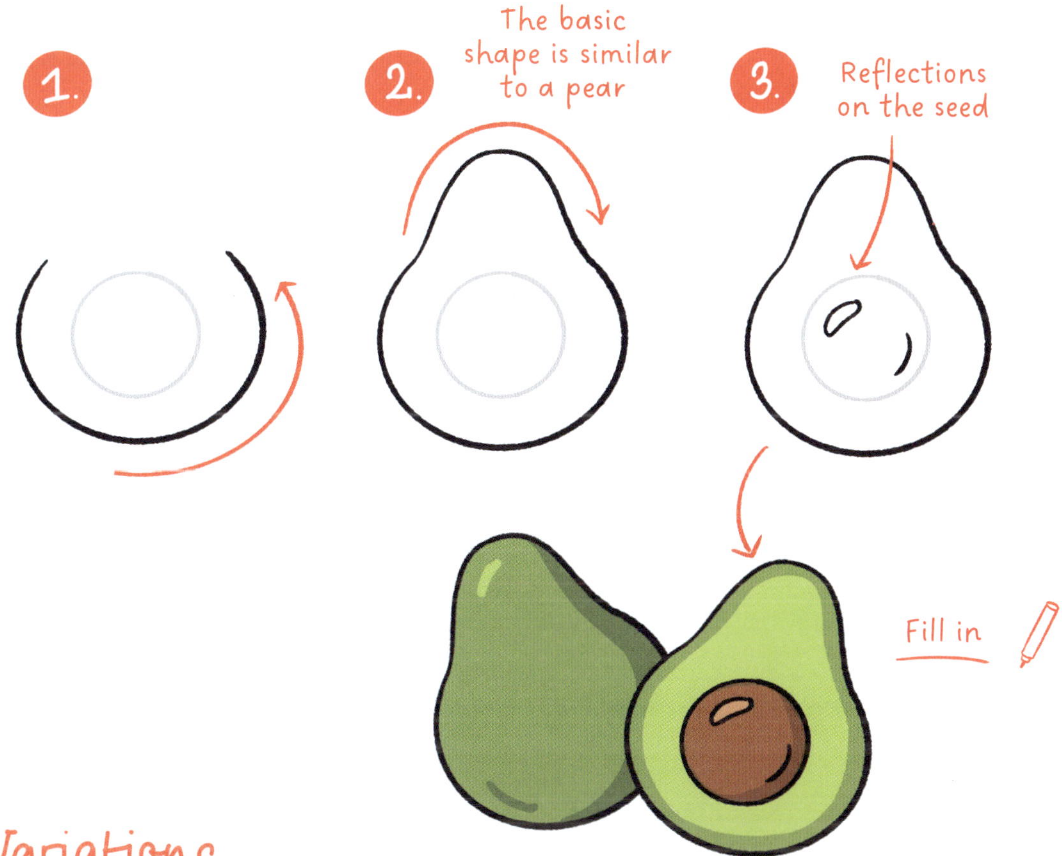

Variations

You can also bring the avocados to life

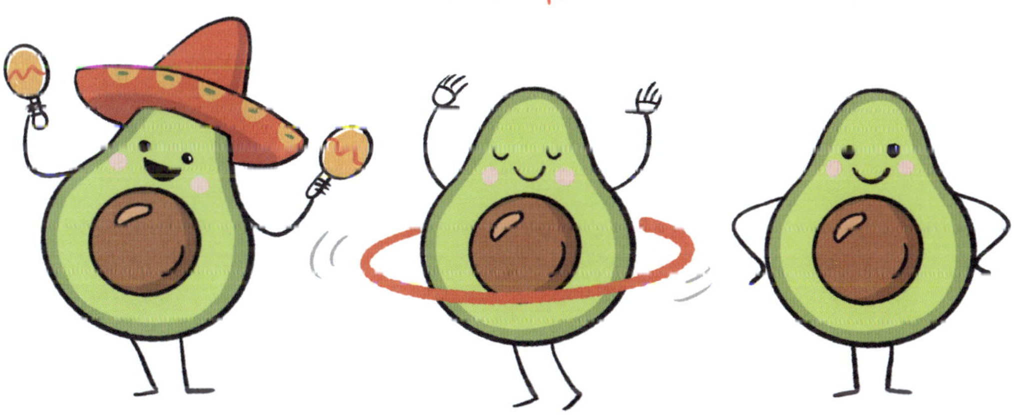

Melon

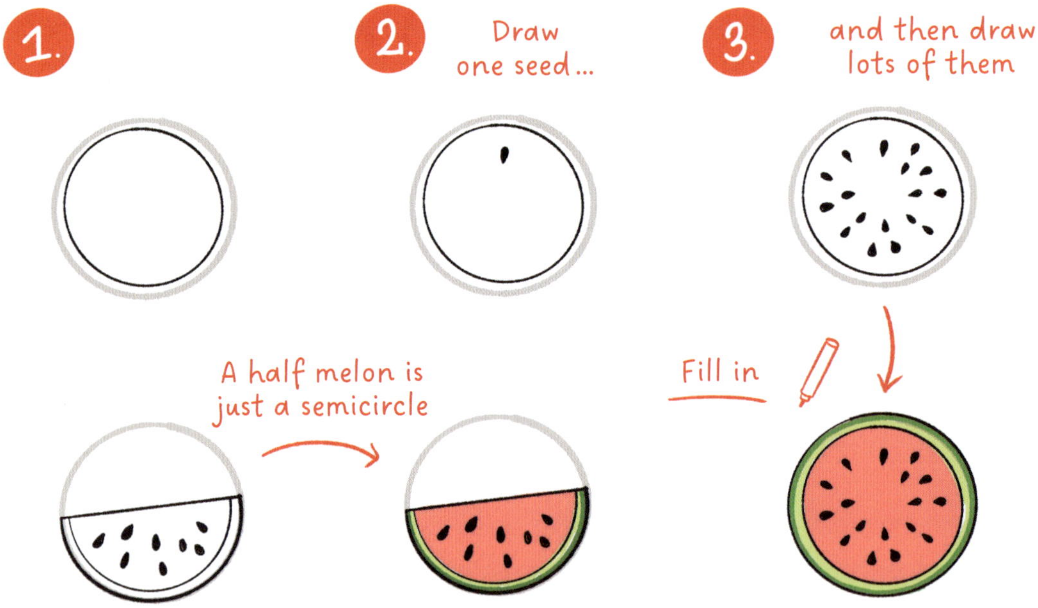
1.
2.
Draw one seed...
3.
and then draw lots of them
A half melon is just a semicircle
Fill in

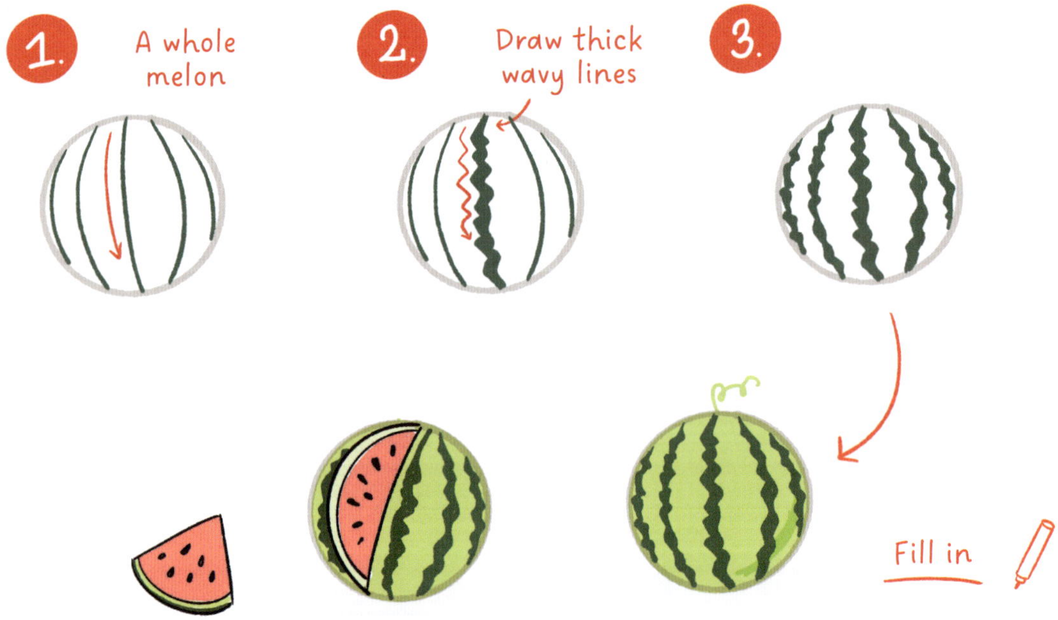
1.
A whole melon
2.
Draw thick wavy lines
3.
Fill in

Orange

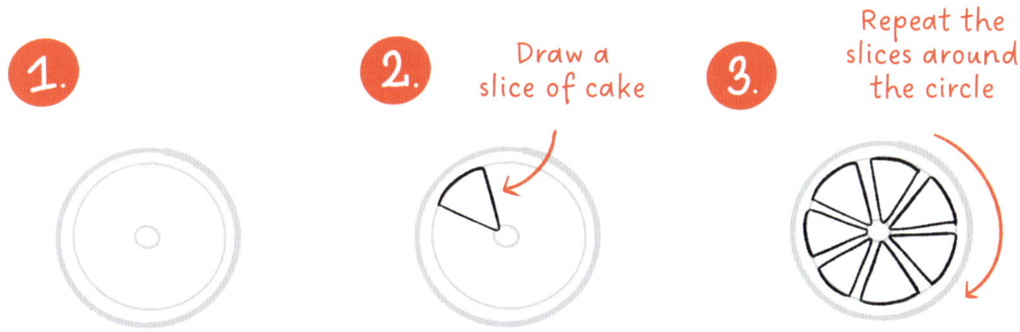
1.
2.
Draw a slice of cake
3.
Repeat the slices around the circle

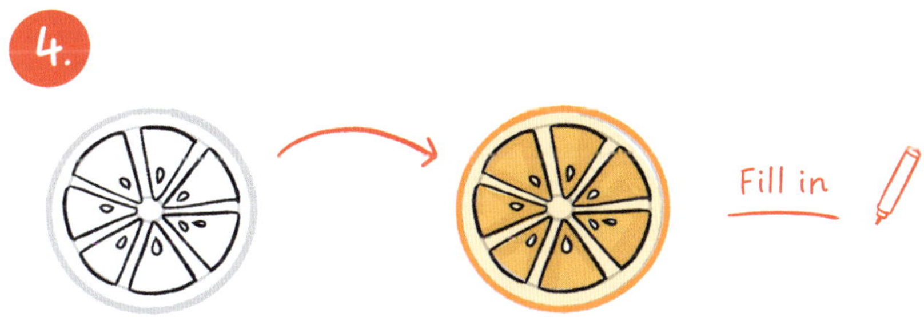
4.
Fill in

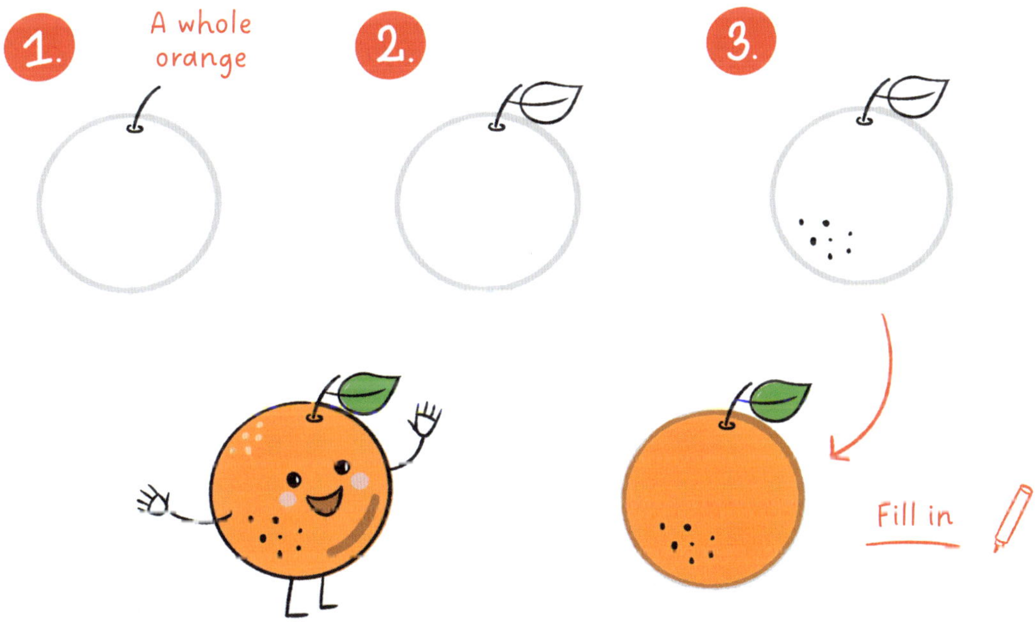
1.
A whole orange
2.
3.
Fill in

Apple

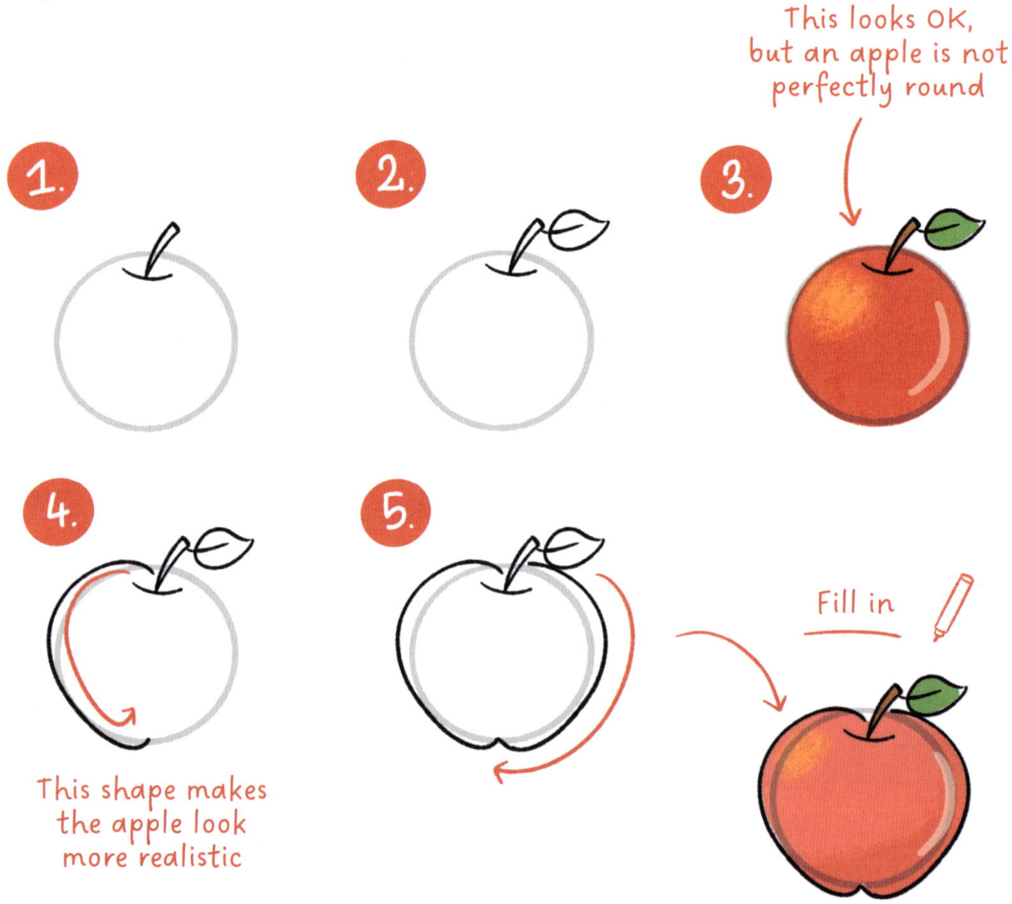

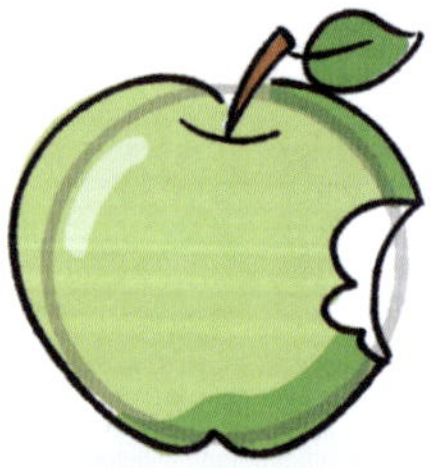

With a bite taken out

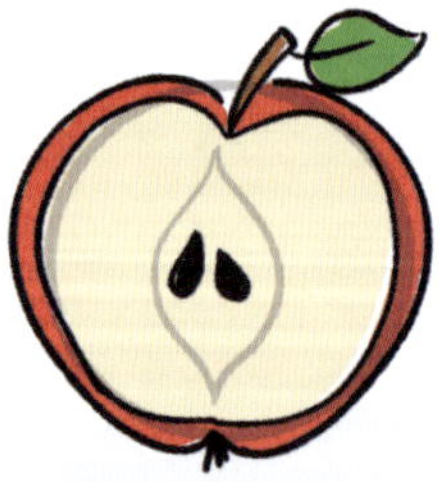

Cross section

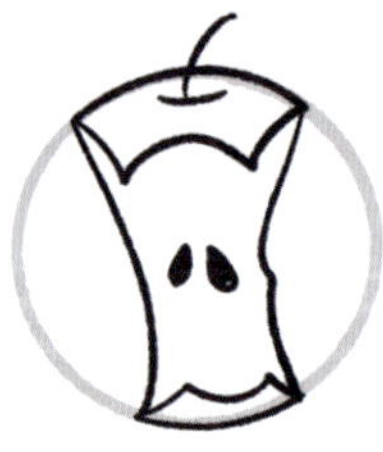

Apple core

Cherry

1.

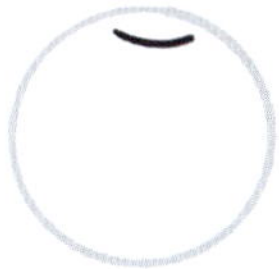

2.

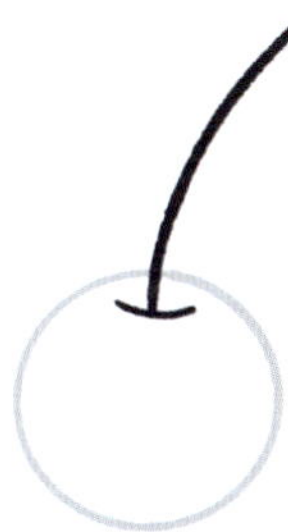

3.

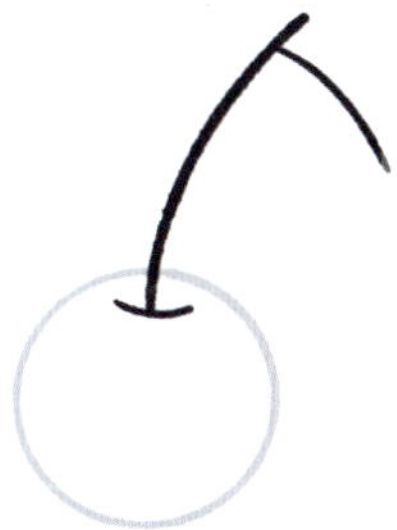

4.

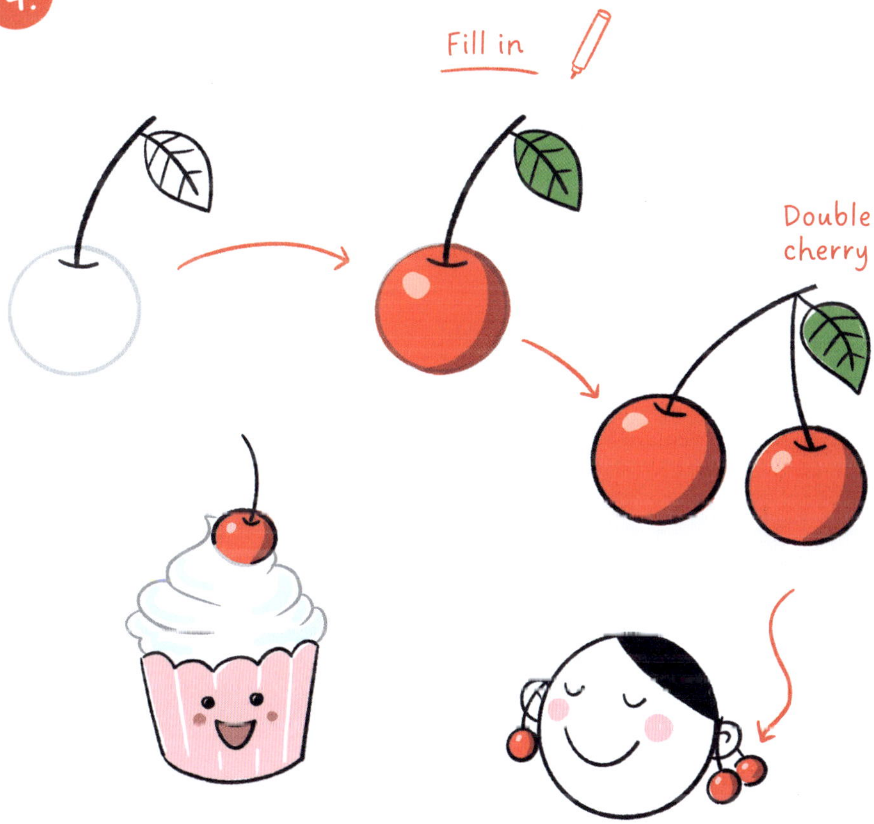

Tomato

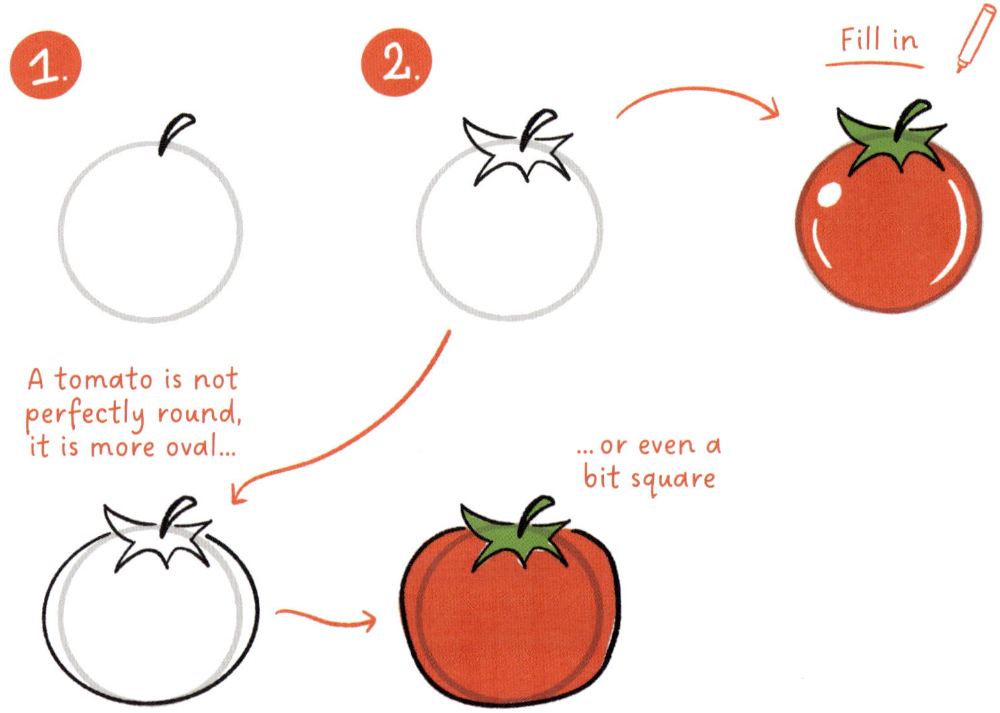

Cut open

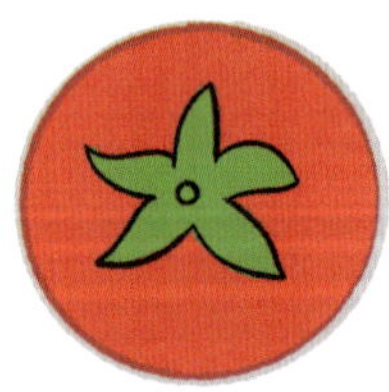

From above

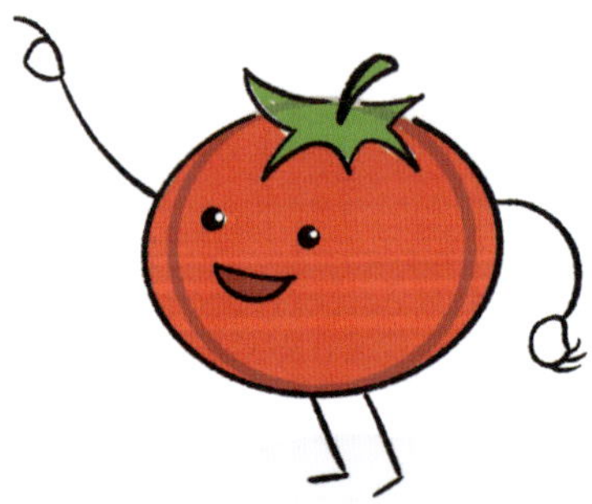

Egg

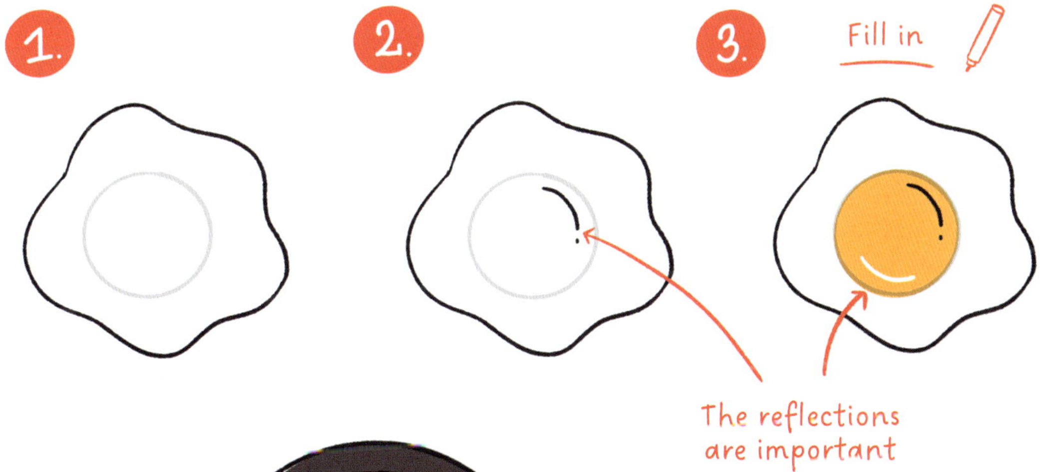

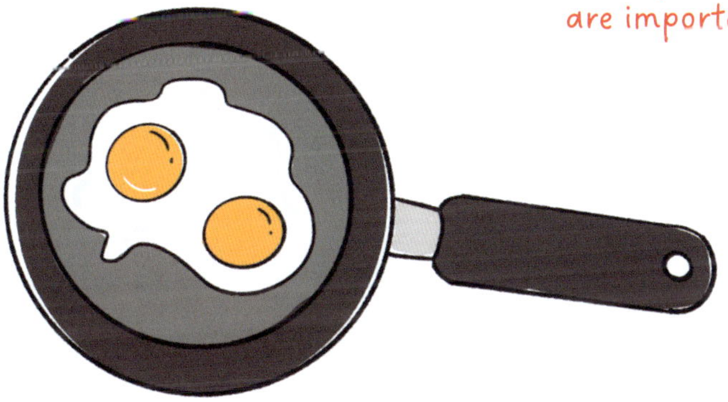

Boiled egg

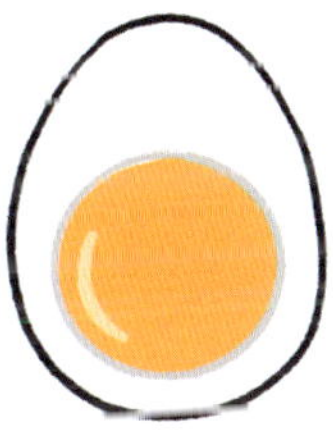

Raw egg

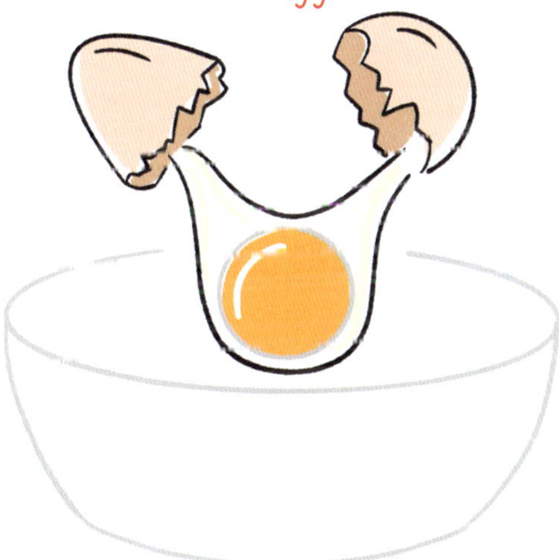

Sushi

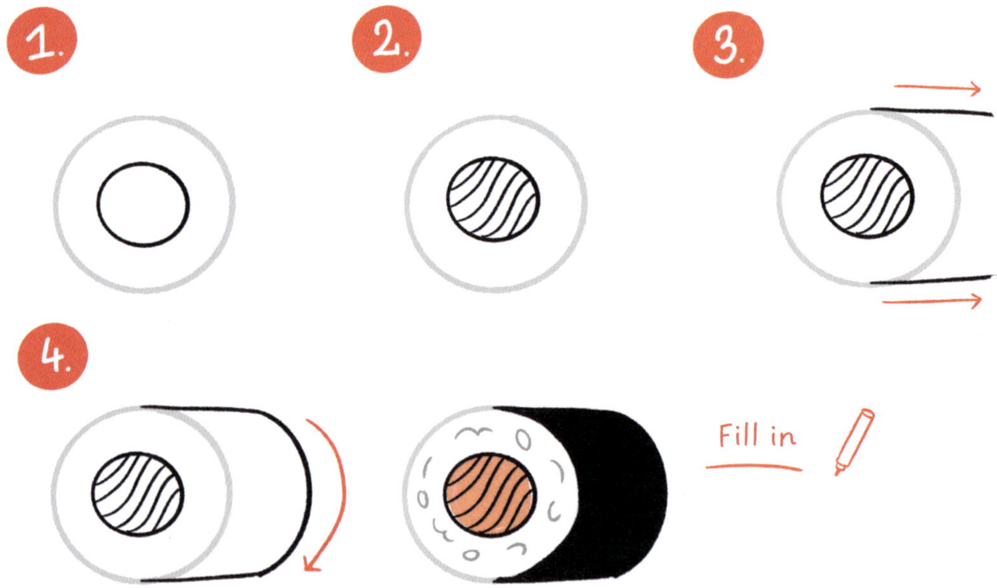
1.
2.
3.
4.
Fill in

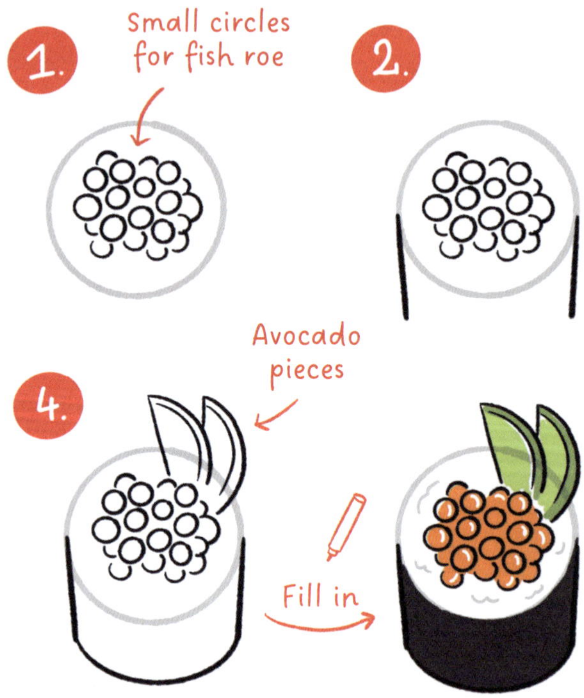
Small circles for fish roe
1.
2.
3.
Avocado pieces
4.
Fill in

Plate (with cutlery)

1.

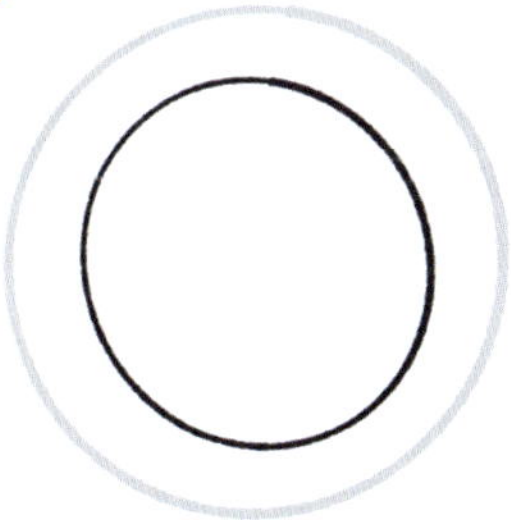

2.

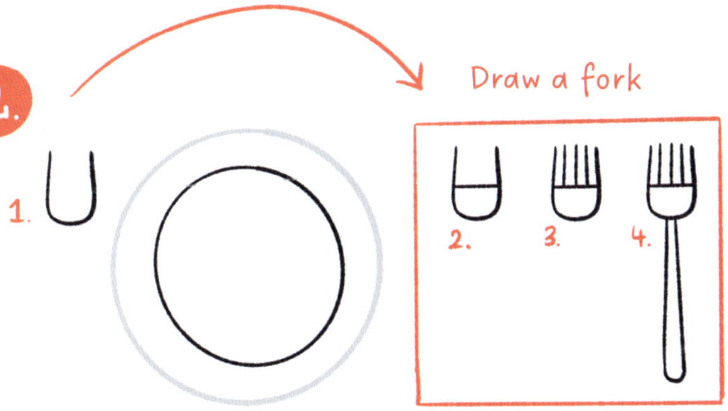

3.

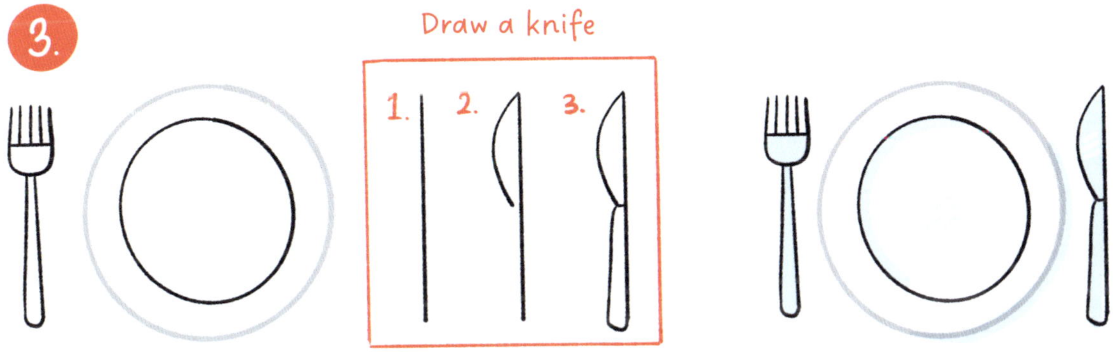

Set the table ◡̈

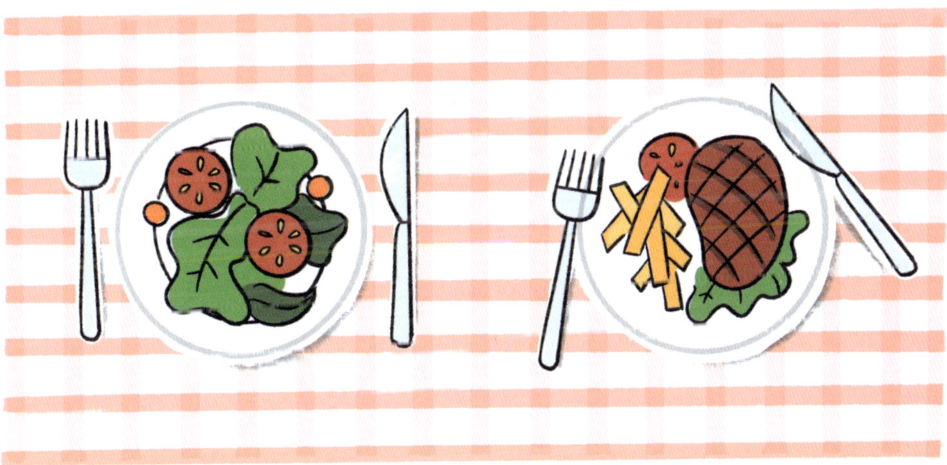

Index

Smith Street Books

Original title: Einfache Dinge aus Kreisen zeichnen by Nadine Rossa © 2025
frechverlag GmbH, Dieselstr. 5, 70839 Gerlingen, Germany a division of
Penguin Random House Verlagsgruppe GmbH, München, Germany.

This edition published in 2026 by Smith Street Books
Naarm (Melbourne) | Australia
smithstreetbooks.com

Distributed outside ANZ, North & Latin America by
Thames & Hudson Ltd
6–24 Britannia Street, London, WC1X 9JD
thamesandhudson.com

EU Authorised Representative: Interart S.A.R.L.
19 rue Charles Auray, 93500 Pantin, Paris, France
productsafety@thameshudson.co.uk; www.interart.fr

ISBN: 978-1-9235-0336-6

All rights reserved. No part of this book may be reproduced or transmitted by any person or entity, in any form or by any means, electronic or mechanical, including photocopying, recording, scanning or by any storage and retrieval system, without the prior written permission of the publishers and copyright holders.

No part of this book may be used or reproduced in any manner for the purpose of training artificial intelligence technologies or systems.

Smith Street Books respectfully acknowledges the Wurundjeri People of the Kulin Nation, who are the Traditional Owners of the land on which we work, and we pay our respects to their Elders past and present.

Copyright text, design and illustrations © Nadine Rossa

The moral right of the author has been asserted.

Publisher: Hannah Koelmeyer
Editor: Lorna Hendry
Proofreader: Pamela Dunne
Prepress: Megan Ellis
Production manager: Aisling Coughlan

Printed & bound in China by C&C Offset Printing Co., Ltd.

Book 473

10 9 8 7 6 5 4 3 2 1

MIX
Paper | Supporting responsible forestry
FSC® C008047
FSC www.fsc.org